This book is dedicated to the people of Elkhart—both past and present—whose faith, determination and courage helped to build a strong foundation for our city's progress and growth, and in doing so made Elkhart a fine place to live, work and play.

The author, advisors, and publisher of this book would like to extend their appreciation to the staff and employees of Key Bank, formerly Ameritrust National Bank, for their support and sponsorship of the initial printing of *Elkhart: A Pictorial History*. Such efforts to record and preserve Elkhart's rich history greatly benefit the present and future citizens of our community. We also with to express our heartfelt thanks to all those who have contributed to this outstanding reflection of our heritage.

Elkhart

A PICTORIAL HISTORY

by George E. Riebs

G. Bradley Publishing, Inc.
St. Louis, Missouri

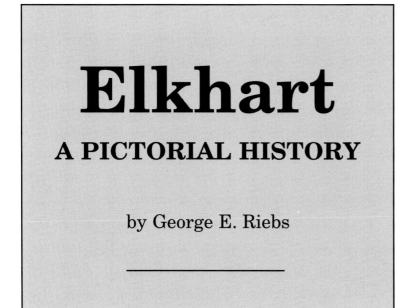

Elkhart

A PICTORIAL HISTORY

by George E. Riebs

PUBLICATION STAFF:
AUTHOR: George E. Riebs
COMMITTEE: Virginia Fluke
      Betty Flitcraft
      Randall L. Adams
      Terry A. Smeltzer
COVER ARTIST: Scott Hendrie
BOOK DESIGN: Diane Kramer
COPY EDITOR: Maija B. Riebs
PUBLISHER: G. Bradley Publishing, Inc.
SPONSOR: Ameritrust National Bank

The advertisements assembled on the inside front and back covers were arranged by Sandra K. Adams and Ruth Adams.

ISBN 0-943963-17-6
Printed in the United States of America

TABLE OF CONTENTS

SOME FIRSTS IN ELKHART

1830 First wedding in Elkhart County (November 11).
1832 First building erected south of the river.
1832 First divorce suit filed in Elkhart County.
1833 First tavern (licensed by Horace Root).
1834 First marriage in Elkhart village (January 2).
1834 First spinning wheel (Mrs. Rosalie Beebe).
1841 First Thanksgiving Day observance in Elkhart County.
1844 First steamboat arrived on St. Joseph River.
1844 First telegraph line.
1850 First piano (Milo Chamberlain).
1851 First sewing machine (Mrs. Louisa Defrees).
1851 First train.
1863 First bank incorporated (First National Bank).
1866 First circulating library (The Ladies' Library).

1867 First roundhouse.
1872 First Opera House (J. L. Broderick).
1875 First Mayor (Henry C. Wright).
1880 First bicycle, a high-wheel (James Ludlow).
1881 First typewriter (F. B. Pratt & Sons).
1895 First player-piano (Harry Goettle).
1896 First "animated pictures" (Peoples Theater).
1898 First Dictaphone (Mennonite Publishing House).
1899 First automobile (James A. Barger).
1899 First electric street lights (August 21).
1903 First one-minute mile in the country! On July 1, Barney Oldfield drove his car, the "Red Devil," one mile in 59.6 seconds.
1906 First horseless carriage (Pratt) made in Elkhart.
1931 First radio station (WJAK) on November 18. It became WTRC a year later.

FOREWORD

So the young "would look back" and their elders "enjoy the memories."

Those are two of the reasons George Riebs gives for taking the readers of "Elkhart — A Pictorial History" on a sentimental journey through Elkhart's yesteryears.

As a social studies teacher for the Elkhart Community Schools, Riebs was challenged to make history more palatable for his young students. How better to help them relate to the past than to mix in the history of their own community?

*"Oh, is that where Elkhart got its name? Pierre Moran
And Christiana Creek?"*

*"Really, can I stand at the very spot of Elkhart's
first settlement? Over 150 years ago?"*

*"There used to be three dime stores in one block on
Main Street—all at the same time? You're kidding?"*

*"At one time, on any day, more than 100 trains would
tie up the Main Street crossing? Awesome!"*

Now, Riebs shares his history lessons with us all — those who remember how it used to be and the youngsters who will be responsible for the continuation of Elkhart's path to prosperity.

That path began as an Indian trail, followed by traders, explorers, and missionaries, and later by spunky men who saw promise of good living in the forests and rich soil at the confluence of two rivers.

The scenery surrounding the St. Joseph and Elkhart rivers has changed over a century and a half . . . from milling and trading center to railroad hub . . . from "band instrument capital of the world" to a worldwide recognition for pharmaceutical and mobile housing manufacturing. Follow that path in *Elkhart — A Pictorial History.*

Foreword by Bettie East
Former Editor of A.M. Magazine
The Elkhart Truth

THE NAME ELKHART

What's in a name? Where did the name of Elkhart come from? While the most popular story is that the Indians noticed the shape of the island (Island Park) at the confluence of the Elkhart and St. Joseph rivers resembled the heart of an elk, evidence strongly suggests that elk did roam this area a very long time ago, it seems more likely (and perhaps just as romantic) that the Elkhart River and Elkhart Prairie (both of which had those names prior to the laying out and naming of the village) were given their names because of the Shawnee Indian Chief Elkhart, who was a cousin of the famous Shawnee Chief Tecumseh. Chief Elkhart and his tribe came into this area from Ohio about 1800, looking for a land with plenty of game, forests, grassy areas, and clear water. Conflicts developed as the Shawnee came into contact with the Ottawa and Potawatomi tribes, who were already here. The ensuing battles were full of intrigue, including the capturing of Chief Elkhart's daughter, Princess Mishawaka, and her eventual marriage to a white scout for the Ottawas, named Dead Shot.

The Miami Indians were the earliest inhabitants of this area. They gave us the name *Mishiwa-Teki-Sipiwi* (meaning Elk-Heart-River), which was later translated by French traders to *Coeur-de-Cerf* (Heart of a Stag). Thus it is quite possible that the second story is true: that Chief Mishiwa-Teki (Elk-Heart) was indeed the father of Princess Mishiwa-ka, and the origin of the name of the city of Elkhart.

The first white men to travel through what is now the city of Elkhart were almost certainly French traders, explorers, or missionaries. Precise details as to the earliest dates and names are few and frequently contradictory, but Father James Marquette and two other French missionaries visited the St. Joseph valley in 1669. The famous explorer, Robert LaSalle, travelled up the River of the Miamis into southeastern Michigan in 1679. Two years later, the river was

continued on pg 10.

Island Park, where the Elkhart River at the right meets the St. Joseph River across the bottom of the picture, is allegedly shaped like the heart of an elk. The bridge at the upper right (southwest) edge of the island connects it to East Sycamore Street.

The original plat of the village of Elkhart by George Crawford in 1832, showing 51 lots.

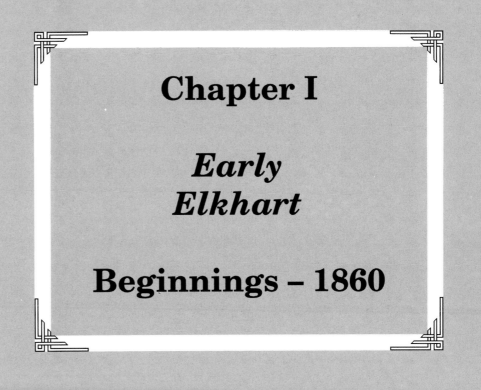

Chapter I

Early Elkhart

Beginnings – 1860

renamed the St. Joseph River. At that time, the location that later became Elkhart was part of New France, claimed in the name of the King of France by LaSalle. The whole area was placed under the jurisdiction of Great Britain by the Treaty of 1763 (following the French and Indian War). It came under the sovereignty of the United States by the Treaty of Paris in 1783, which formally ended our Revolutionary War.

The Potawatomi Indians moved into this area about 1700, pushing out most of the Miamis. As early as 1779, letters and other records refer to the Potawatomi village of Coeur de Cerf.

When Samuel Bibbins visited the present site of Elkhart in 1800, he found only two white men. They were French traders who were trying to barter with the local Indians. William Johnston, travelling through the county in 1809, stated that the place where the Elkhart and St. Joseph rivers meet was ideally suited by nature to be the location of a city. In 1822 the Rev. Isaac McCoy and his wife, Christiana, encamped on the Elkhart River on their way to the Carey Baptist Mission near Niles, Michigan, and Rev. McCoy named Christiana Creek after his wife.

Meanwhile, the United States was pushing its geographical boundaries farther west. The Northwest Ordinance of 1787 established the Northwest Territory, which included the present states of Ohio, Indiana, Michigan, Illinois, Wisconsin, and part of

LaSalle and fellow explorers near the St. Joseph-Kankakee portage in 1679 in what is now South Bend.

Map of the old Northwest Territory (including the Elkhart area when it was still part of New France) made by a British cartographer in England in 1721. The "St. Joseph River of the Miamis" extends diagonally to the southeast from Lake Michigan, just to the left of the words, "the Potowatamis."

Reverand Issac McCoy

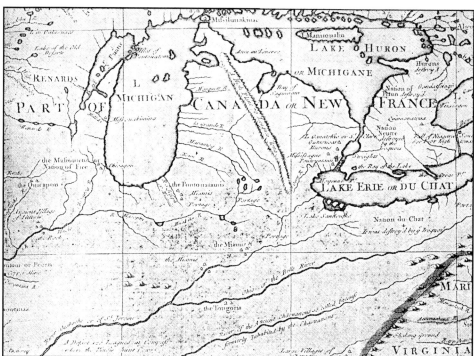

Minnesota. In 1803 Ohio became the first state formed out of the Northwest Territory, with the remainder being called the Indiana Territory. Two years later, the Michigan Territory was officially organized, with its southern boundary being a line from the southern tip of Lake Michigan eastward to Lake Erie. This included the present locations of Michigan City, South Bend, Elkhart, and Toledo, Ohio.

When war broke out between the United States and Great Britain in 1812, the British, from their position in Canada, captured Detroit, and claimed all of Michigan Territory to be part of Canada (British North America). A year later, General William Henry Harrison, later to become the ninth President of the United States, led an army that recaptured Detroit and reinstated this area as part of Michigan Territory. In 1816 Indiana was admitted as a state and declared its northern boundary to be a line ten miles north of the southern tip of Lake Michigan, in order to provide for the possibility of having a port on Lake Michigan in the future. Congress approved the border shift, and thus Elkhart eventually became a city in Indiana, instead of in Michigan.

Five years later, on August 29, 1821, an Indian Treaty was signed at Chicago that played a significant part in the history of the city of Elkhart. Three thousand Indians from the Ottawa, Chippewa, and Potawatomi tribes attended. The United States was

Christiana McCoy

The Northwest Territory in 1787.

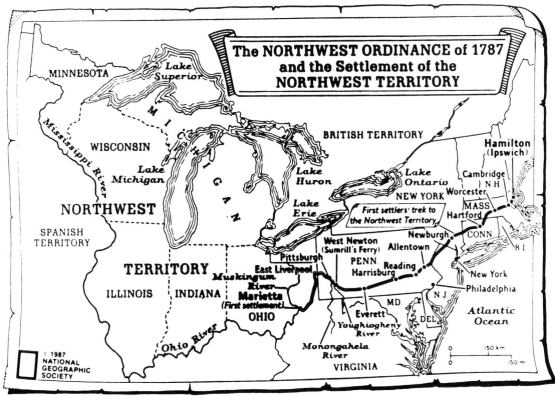

represented by Commissioners Lewis Cass and Solomon Sibley. One of the witnesses at the signing of the treaty was Gabriel Godfroy, an Indian Agent. At this treaty one section of land, Section 5 of Concord Township in Elkhart County, Indiana, was awarded to an Indian named Pierre Moran. The boundaries of Section 5 are formed on the north by a line crossing Main Street just north of the Main Street bridge (about where Christiana Creek crosses Main Street); on the east by a line connecting Johnson Street and Prairie Street; on the south by a line crossing Main Street at the railroad tracks; and on the west by a line going along Michigan Street.

Pierre Moran was the son of a Frenchman,

Constant Moran, and a Kickapoo Indian squaw. He was born about the time of the Revolutionary War and died about 1840. Raised in Warren County, he eventually became a Kickapoo Chief and was involved in the Battle of Tippecanoe in 1811. Apparently he was blamed for the loss of the battle, perhaps because he was only half Indian. At any rate, he was kicked out by the Kickapoo tribe, headed north, and married a Potawatomi woman, joining her tribe and becoming a Potawatomi Chief.

In 1827 Richard Godfroy, son of Gabriel Godfroy, approached Pierre Moran with an offer to buy his land. He said he would pay the Indian chief $300 for all of Section 5 (640 acres). However, Godfroy, being a

The ten-mile strip between the solid and dotted lines, including what is now Elkhart, was transferred from Michigan Territory to Indiana in 1816 in order that Indiana might be able to have a port on Lake Michigan.

An 1812 map of the Michiana area, showing Lake Michigan, Green Bay (top left), Lake Huron (top right), and the St. Joseph River (shaped like a fish hook) with the "Elksheart River" branching off due east. The confluence of these two rivers is the location of Island Park. The original of this map is in the National Archives at Washington, D. C.

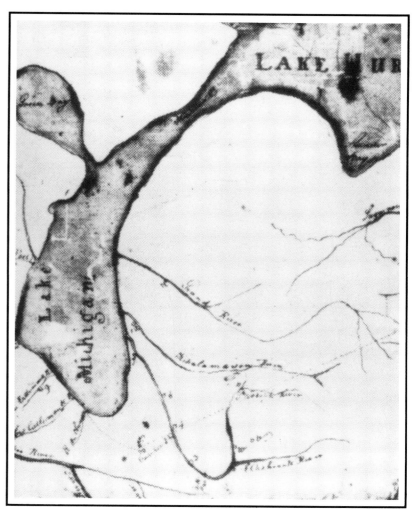

little short of cash, gave Pierre Moran a horse and wagon, which he claimed was worth $112, as a down payment, promising to pay the remaining $188 later.

During this time, the first white settlers appeared in what is now Elkhart. While various sources differ as to the exact dates, it seems that Andrew Noffsinger was the first settler, locating on the north bank of the St. Joseph River near the present site of the Sherman Street bridge as early as 1821 and staying till about 1828. Jesse Rush arrived in early 1827, settled near Noffsinger, and then moved south of Elkhart to Pleasant Plain in early 1828, where his wife gave birth to twins on May 16. And so it was that Isaiah Rush became the first settler child born in Elkhart

County, followed moments later by his twin sister, Marjorie. In October of 1835, John H. Broderick became the first settler child born in the village of Elkhart. His parents, Nehemiah F. and Margaret L. Broderick, are buried in Grace Lawn Cemetery.

George Crawford settled near the mouth of Christiana Creek in 1828, not long before Lewis Davis and Chester Sage. Shortly after their arrival, they built a grist mill close to the mouth of Christiana Creek. This settlement was called Pulaski, in honor of the Polish general who gave his life in the service of George Washington during our Revolutionary War. The post office which was established at Pulaski in 1829 kept its name after moving south of the St.

Fort Dearborn, in Chicago, as it appeared in 1816. Here, in 1821, the Indian treaty was signed, awarding Section 5 to Pierre Moran.

Map of Section 5, Concord Township, Elkhart County, State of Indiana. This land was given to Pierre Moran by the Indian Treaty of 1821 at Chicago, and sold to Dr. Havilah Beardsley in 1831 for $1,500.

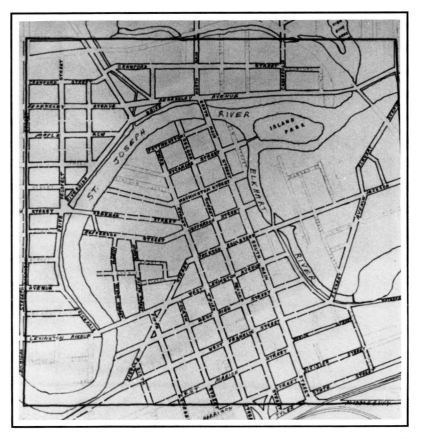

Joseph River to the newer village of Elkhart. The name of the post office was officially changed to Elkhart in 1839.

In 1830, having heard how beautiful the St. Joseph valley was, Dr. Havilah Beardsley arrived on horseback, settling temporarily in Pulaski with George Crawford. Realizing the potential of the water power provided by three streams coming together there, he decided that he would like to buy the land, offering Pierre Moran $800. When this offer was submitted to John Tipton, the Indian Agent, Tipton insisted the land was worth $1500. Beardsley agreed that this was a fair price, and on April 21, 1831, a deed was drawn up between Pierre Moran and Havilah Beardsley.

During this period in our country's history, the signature of the President of the United States was required on the deed of any land sold by an Indian to a white man. Historians disagree as to whether Godfroy ever got the President's signature, but at least one source claimed that President John Quincy Adams had approved and signed Godfroy's deed on November 28, 1826. Regardless, Tipton said that Godfroy had not offered to pay one fourth of the value of the land, and therefore his claim to ownership of the land was not valid. In fact, there is no evidence to suggest that Godfroy ever paid the remaining $188 of his agreement.

A further complication arose because homes and mills had already been built by a number of settlers on the disputed land. Dr. Beardsley agreed to give

Isaiah Rush, son of Jesse and Mary Rush. He was born on May 16, 1828, the first white settler baby born in Elkhart County.

Nehemiah F. Broderick was the first school teacher in Elkhart. His school was a log cabin located on East Washington Street close to the Elkhart River. In October, 1835, his wife, Margaret, gave birth to a son, John, the first settler child born in the village of Elkhart.

Godfroy a portion of land equal in value to the $112 which he had paid to Pierre Moran. On January 13, 1832, President Andrew Jackson approved and signed the deed making Dr. Havilah Beardsley the sole owner of the land that became the heart of the city of Elkhart. In 1832, Dr. Beardsley hired George Crawford to plat the first 51 lots for the village of Elkhart, bounded by Pigeon Street (later Lexington Avenue) on the south, by Washington Street on the north, by the Elkhart River on the east, and by the alley between Second Street and what later became Third Street on the west. With this accomplished, the city of Elkhart (as we know it today) had begun to take shape.

Historical marker at the site of the settlement of Pulaski, near the mouth of the Christiana Creek on East Beardsley Avenue, just west of Johnson Street.

Dr. Havilah Beardsley, founder of Elkhart.

Rachael Calhoun Beardsley, wife of Havilah, cousin of Vice-President John C. Calhoun.

The old Beardsley paper mill, built by Havilah Beardsley in 1846, burned down in 1874 and was replaced by this brick structure the same year. It was operated by members of the Beardsley family until 1890, when it was leased to other operators. Fires in 1900 and 1909 finally destroyed the building. Though there has been much confusion regarding the location of Havilah Beardsley's paper mill and flour mill on Riverside Drive (originally called Front Street), this is the mill that was located at the foot of Edwardsburg Road, where it meets Riverside Drive. Children used to play in the ruins of this mill's raceway as late as the 1950's.

The Beardsley flour mill, long a landmark in Elkhart, was built in 1840 on North Riverside Drive, just west of the intersection of Beardsley Avenue and Riverside Drive, about 100 yards upstream of the Beardsley paper mill. This mill was dismantled in 1904. For five years, a huge reproduction of this mill adorned the main drop curtain of the Bucklen Opera House.

Alexander Arisman

The old Arisman saw mill, about 1885, located at the mouth of Christiana Creek on the north bank of the St. Joseph River. This mill was built about 1868, replacing the original saw mill, which had been built by Havilah Beardsley in 1831.

The residence of Dr. and Mrs. Havilah Beardsley, built in 1848, is still located on its original site at the northwest corner of Main Street and Beardsley Avenue. It was the first brick house built north of the St. Joseph River. A tunnel connecting the house to the river was partially filled when Beardsley Avenue was paved. It was feared that increased traffic weight would cause a cave-in. Some people think that this tunnel was part of an Underground Railroad station used to transport slaves to freedom, but the only Underground Railroad stations in Elkhart County were located along State Road 15, including one in Bristol.

The old W. B. Vanderlip home, on the northwest corner of Second and Harrison streets. Built in 1866, this house was moved to 212 West Harrison in 1904. It was torn down in 1957 when the underpass was being built. Other homes built about the same time as the Vanderlip home may still be seen around Elkhart. They can be easily identified by the unique architectural styling around the tops of the windows. The Winchester mansion was built on this corner in 1906 and is still there, but it is sometimes called the Knickerbocker mansion.

The "Shot Tower," located on the northwest corner of Second and High streets, was built in 1835 and was the Howard Ogle residence. Later it became Elkhart's first armory. It was purchased by A. R. Beardsley in 1911, then torn down and replaced by the present Municipal Building in 1915. The nickname of "Shot Tower" came from the fact that the ground originally sloped sharply downward on the north side of the building giving the appearance of a three-story structure. This reminded someone of the old shot towers, from the top of which molten lead was dropped into a container of cool water. The "shot" was then sold by grocers as ammunition. Even though there is no evidence that this building was a shot tower, the nickname remained for many years.

"The Elkhart House," originally called "The American," was one of the first hotels in Elkhart, and was built on the southeast corner of Second Street and Jackson Boulevard in 1843, and torn down in 1910. It was a regular stop for the stagecoach from Toledo to Chicago. Willard F. Wickwire became the proprietor in 1860 and lived there with his wife until he died in 1899. Wickwire displayed a sign, painted by W. B. Vanderlip, that showed an elk's head on a flaming heart. At one time "The American" was the scene of many social functions and dances. Boarders were called to dinner by a large triangle hung on the roof, rather than the bell or gong used by most boarding houses. Rates in 1860 ran from $1.50 to $2.00 per day, with "free hack to and from all trains."

"Tammany Hall," built on the southwest corner of Main and Jefferson streets in 1836, was later called the "Bee Hive" because of all the activity that went on in it. The first church services in Elkhart were held there as the Baptists organized in 1836. In addition, there were temperance lectures, amateur theatrical performances, and many other types of entertainment. It was originally built to be a tavern by Henry L. Slater.

Philo Morehous settled in Elkhart in 1842, when the population of the village was about 300. In 1854 he founded the first bank in town, the Bank of Elkhart, which became the First National Bank (in 1864) and Ameritrust National Bank (in 1989).

This is a sketch of the Commercial Block on the west side of Main Street, just south of Jackson Boulevard, in 1860. Stores located in this block were owned and operated by John McNaughton, William Brooks, J. Primly, J. Davenport, and Samuel Strong. These stores extended from the corner of Jackson Boulevard to the first alley south on Main Street. Together with the stores across the street on Main Street and the stores just around the corner on West Jackson Boulevard., they comprised the heart of the business district in Elkhart in the early 1860's.

Tombstone of Martha Ann Keltner, wife of George W. Keltner, found in Ox Bow Park Cemetery. Martha died September 16, 1846, at the age of 17. Her husband, who was 23 at the time of her death, married Arminda M. Wilson in 1855. He died May 18, 1858, and was buried in Burkette Cemetery, Elkhart.

Douglas Beardsley and Ed Faber bet on the national election of 1872, in which Ulysses S. Grant beat Horace Greeley. Beardsley won the bet, and on November 22, 1872, with snow on the ground, Faber had to wheel him to Goshen in a light wheelbarrow built especially for the occasion. Beardsley's liquor business was still located on Division Street as late as 1874.

Ed Miller, proprietor of Clifton House, won a bet from Mike Kaskel on the Presidential election of 1892 (Grover Cleveland beat Benjamin Harrison). Kaskel, who owned a cigar store next door had to push Miller from Bristol to the hotel in this wheelbarrow. Miller wore a silk hat, cut-away coat, and diamonds, and smoked a cigar while being pushed. This wheelbarrow appears to be the same one as the one in which Douglas Beardsley rode. It was displayed for many years in Russell's tavern, until it was sold at auction in 1985.

Kavanagh and Pollard's Elkhart Palace grocery store, located on the southwest corner of Main and High streets, was built in the early 1860's for Hiram Goodspeed, and was originally used as a wagon shop. After the wagon business was moved to another location, a man by the name of Regue opened a grocery store in this building. Later, Americus Goodspeed (Hiram's son) and James Kavanagh (Hiram's son-in-law) opened a grocery store there. In a few months, Goodspeed sold his share to John B. Pollard, who was a former fellow worker of Kavanagh's in the Lake Shore machine shop. When Kavanagh died in 1906, his son, John, took his place until 1916, the year Pollard died. The store was then closed and sold to C. G. Conn, who later sold it to H. E. Bucklen. In April, 1917, the First National Bank purchased the property from the Bucklen estate, tore down the old structure, and built a new bank building there. Today Ameritrust National Bank still occupies the same corner, though the building and the services offered have been greatly expanded and modernized.

Russell's tavern, located on the south side of the 100 block of west Jackson Blvd. At the time it closed, due to Robert Russell's death in 1985, it was the oldest tavern continuously owned and operated by one family in the state of Indiana, having begun in 1872.

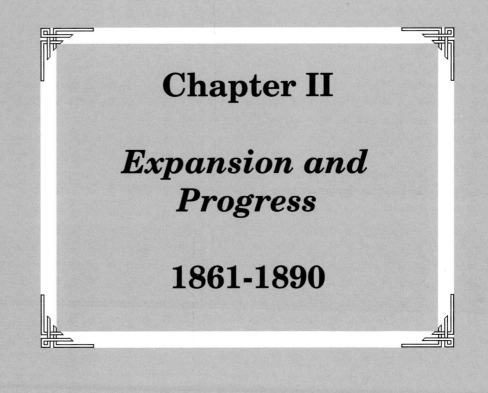

Chapter II

Expansion and Progress

1861-1890

Elkhart experienced a great deal of growth during the period between the beginning of the Civil War and 1890. The population increased nearly 800%, from about 1500 to 11,360. The rapid expansion of the railroad was responsible for part of that increase. As the first roundhouse and railroad repair shops were built here in 1867 to 1871, and the number of railroad jobs grew rapidly, many workers from Italy and from down South moved to Elkhart with their families,.

In 1868 the first dam was built over the St. Joseph River, increasing the number of factories and mills which could be operated by hydraulic power. Nine new schools were opened in Elkhart during this period, to keep up with the rapid growth in the population of school-aged children. The first post office building was built, and many church denominations were established or expanded. In 1875, by a narrow margin, Elkhart voted to become a city. However, in 1880 lamp lighters were still needed each evening to light the gas or oil street lamps, and to turn them out each morning. There were no sewers, pavements, telephones, electric lights, or water works, as of yet. The only public utility was the gas works.

The 1880's brought further changes. It was during this time that the Bucklen Opera House and the Bucklen Hotel were opened, and C.G. Conn began his band instrument factory, which after a major fire, rebounded into an even bigger manufacturing company than before. A number of newspapers came and went, but the *Elkhart Truth,* begun in 1889, outlasted them all. Main Street was paved with cedar blocks, and at first horse-drawn, and later electric, streetcars were introduced. The water works was established, sewer lines were put in, and cisterns and wells were filled, because they were no longer needed.

Most workers in the 1880's worked ten hours per day, six days per week. Common laborers were paid $1.25 per day, while skilled workers received as much as twice that amount. For entertainment, there were Gypsy camps, medicine shows, and circus performances at Johnson Commons, near the west end of Pigeon Street bridge. Although there were no motion picture shows, road companies presented stage productions at the Broderick Opera House, on the second floor of 125-127 South Main Street, until the opening of the Bucklen Opera House. Even though these were referred to as the horse and buggy days, most of the travel was done on foot, since very few people owned horses and buggies. For this reason, many people chose to live near their work, accounting for the clusters of houses on both sides of the railroad tracks and near the various factories and stores in town. The only bicycles in Elkhart in the 1880's were the kind with one high wheel and one small wheel, and with narrow tires. There were five or six of these in town. The first "safety" bicycle in Elkhart (with two wheels of equal size) arrived in 1890, and drew a great deal of attention.

Taken during the Civil War, this picture shows the encampment of Company C of the 9th Indiana Volunteers (Jesse Drake's company).

This picture of Jesse B. Drake was taken in 1865, immediately after his return to Elkhart from the Civil War. He had been a private in Company C of the 9th Indiana Volunteers, having fought in the battle at Stone River, and in at least 20 other battles. He was taken prisoner at the battle of Chickamauga, and held for 18 months, then exchanged for a Confederate soldier shortly before the war's end. Drake married Elizabeth Heasley in 1869. They had three children, one of whom was Charles S. Drake, owner of Drake's department store.

Many other soldiers from Elkhart fought in the Civil War. C. G. Conn, Ambrose Bierce, Capt. Orville Chamberlain, and Col. Ruel Johnson were only a few. Lt. Frank Baldwin was killed in the battle of Stone River. Indiana was also represented in the battle of Gettysburg, by at least three regiments (the 19th, 20th, and 27th). Hoosiers were involved in the battles of Shiloh, The Wilderness, and Appomattox, to name just a few.

"By direction of the President " (McKinley), Captain Orville T. Chamberlain, of Company G, 74th Indiana Infantry, is cited for "being exposed to a galling fire going in search of another regiment, finding its location, procuring ammunition from the men thereof, and returning with such ammunition to your own company." With these words, Chamberlain was awarded the Congressional Medal of Honor, for distinguished gallantry at the battle of Chickamauga, on September 20, 1863. He was barely 21 years old when the battle occurred, and to date is the only citizen of Elkhart to have received a Congressional Medal of Honor.

This is a picture of the Elkhart Cornet Band, taken shortly after the Civil War.

Elkhartans turning out to give local soldiers an enthusiastic send-off. The soldiers were leaving for the Spanish-American War, in the spring of 1898. This view is looking east on Harrison Street, from the 800 block.

Churches...

On the right side is the first building erected for St. Vincent's Catholic Church (in 1868), just south of the present church on South Main Street. The rectory on the left was built in 1871.

The present St. Vincent's Church was built in 1887 on the southeast corner of Main and Prairie, while the Rev, Jeremiah H. Quinlan was pastor. In 1878 the parochial school was started to the south of the church.

First Baptist Church, built on the southwest corner of Third Street and Lexington Avenue in 1860, had the distinction of being the oldest church building in the city when it was torn down in 1977. Baptists first met in "Tammany Hall" as early as 1836. The organization of the present congregation began in 1859 through the efforts of Rev. Loyle A. Alford, who came here from Hillsdale, Michigan. Oil lights and wood-burning stoves were replaced in 1891 by gas lights and a furnace. The church building was sold to Calvary Assembly of God in 1957, and a new church was built by the Baptists at the corner of Hively and Prairie.

The Christian Science Church, built on the southeast corner of Second and Lexington in 1916, was first organized in Elkhart in 1887. As with many other churches here, the first services were held in private homes. Later, services were moved to the Bucklen Opera House building. A Christian Science Reading Room was opened in a residence at Fourth and Lexington in 1897. By 1904 increased attendance caused the church and reading room to be moved to the second floor of a new building at 111 West Lexington. The building shown here, designed by local architect E. Hill Turnock, was opened for services in early 1918. A new church was built at 2913 East Bristol Street in 1981, and the old building was torn down in 1984.

The German Lutheran Church was built on the northeast corner of Third and Harrison streets in 1912. It was later known as the Evangelical Lutheran Church. The congregation was organized in 1889 and built its first church at Eden and Prairie streets. Services were originally conducted in German, with English services held on alternate weeks in 1923. The last German service was held in 1954. A merger with the Congregational church in 1957 caused its name to be changed to St. John's United Church of Christ. Five years later the congregation moved to the present site at 2701 East Bristol Street. At the time this picture was taken, Third Street (at left) was not yet paved. The church was torn down in 1973, and replaced by a small park.

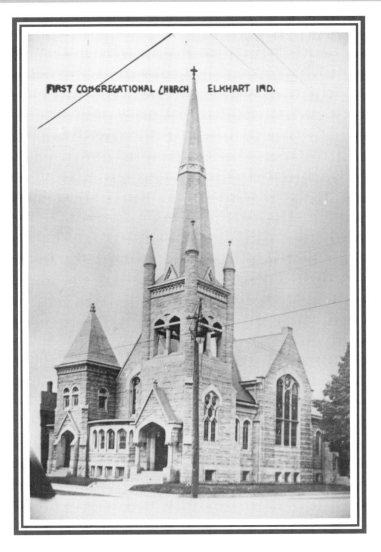

First Congregational Church, as well as several other churches, held many of its earliest services in "Tammany Hall," on the southwest corner of Main and Jefferson streets.

In May of 1844 the Congregational and Presbyterian churches formed a "Plan of Union" and shared in the construction and use of the wooden church built on the southeast corner of Second and High streets. However, by 1869 the growth in membership of both churches made separation necessary. Early in 1870 an agreement was reached to allow Congregational services to be held in First Baptist Church for two years, until a new building could be built on the northeast corner of Fourth and Marion streets. Continued growth brought about the need in 1907 to construct the church in this picture, on the northwest corner of Third and Marion streets. In 1967 this church was torn down and replaced by a new one at the same location.

While the first services of St. John's Episcopal Church were held in Dr. and Mrs. Joseph Chamberlain's home as early as 1845, it was not until 1867 that the first resident pastor (Rev. M. V. Averill) was appointed. In 1873 a small frame church was built at the northeast corner of Third and Pigeon (Lexington) streets. Twenty-two years later the need of larger facilities became obvious. The little church building was moved to the northwest corner of Third and Marion streets. Some time later it was moved to 1128 Johnson Street, and has been used by several other churches. While awaiting the completion of their new church, the Episcopalians met for a while in the G. A. R. hall on Jackson Boulevard, behind Danforth Drug Store (located on the southwest corner of Main and Jackson). The first service in the present church was held on July 5, 1896. The building is made of native fieldstone, most of it from the old Redfield Farm (the owners of the farm were in-laws of H. E. Bucklen). It is considered the only example of Gothic architecture in Elkhart. This picture was taken about 1905, when Third Street was not yet paved.

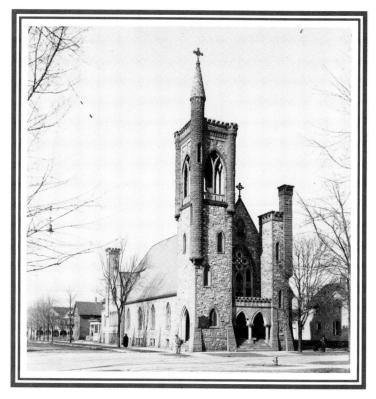

The first Mennonite to arrive in Elkhart was John F. Funk. A former Chicago lumber dealer, he came here in 1867 and organized the Mennonite Publishing Company. By 1871 there were enough Mennonites in Elkhart to construct the church building on Prairie Street. After additions in 1895 and 1901, the church looked like it does in this picture. In 1931 this building was destroyed by fire and replaced shortly thereafter with the present church.

In 1829 the first "circuit riding" Methodist preachers came through what is now Elkhart, giving the Methodists the first official church representation in the new settlement. The first regular meetings were held in the log cabin of James Bannon on the northeast corner of Second and Jefferson. Until 1855 the Methodists met in various homes and other public buildings, including "Tammany Hall." The first Trinity Methodist Episcopal Church was built over a seven year period, beginning in 1855. Due to three separate, violent storms which caused severe damage, it was not completed until 1862. The construction work was done almost entirely by men of the congregation during their "spare time," after working ten to twelve hours per day on their regular jobs. The first organ was not added until 1872, due in part to a dispute between conservative and progressive members over whether or not "too worldly" an instrument should be taken into the church. By 1887 the congregation had grown so much that plans were drawn up for a new building, even though some members left to form a new branch, Willowdale Methodist, in 1888. (This new branch later became St. Paul's Methodist Church.) In 1889 the Trinity Methodist Church in this picture was torn down to make way for a larger building.

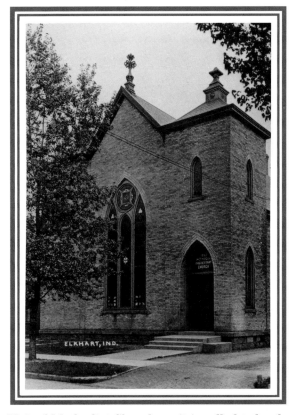

Grace United Methodist Church, as it is called today, located at 137 Division Street, has occupied the same site since the church was first organized in 1893. Originally called the Independent Evangelical Church, its name was changed to Grace Methodist Protestant Church shortly before the dedication of the church building in September, 1894.

The Presbyterian congregation was organized in 1840 in the Beebe home at the northwest corner of Main and Jackson. Later, the Presbyterians met in "Tammany Hall" and, in a "Plan of Union" with the Congregationalists, built a small wooden church on the southeast corner of Second and High streets in 1844. As the two congregations continued to grow, a separation became necessary in 1869, which left the church building with the Presbyterians. In 1872 the brick structure shown here was completed, replacing the old wooden one. Originally the entrance was on the north side, with the pews facing south. In 1885 the entrance was moved to the west side, and the pulpit was relocated on the east side. For many years, the bell in the steeple of this church served as the community firebell, until the firehouse got its own. Growth in membership resulted in this building being torn down in April, 1909, to make way for the new domed church.

The domed First Presbyterian Church, located on the southeast corner of Second and High, was designed by E. Hill Turnock and was completed in 1910. After a study of necessary renovations in 1954 the decision to build a new church was made. In 1960 the present church on East Beardsley Avenue was completed. The domed church was then torn down to make way for the new Elkhart Public Library.

Long a landmark in downtown Elkhart, this second Trinity Methodist Church was located on the same site as the first one, just south of the alley on the west side of Second Street between High and Franklin. It was built in 1889 and used until 1961, when the congregation moved to a new edifice at 2715 East Jackson Boulevard. This building was sold to Elkhart High School and used by the school until 1972 when it was replaced by the Elkhart County court building.

Canaan Baptist Church, the first black Baptist church in Elkhart, was founded in 1918, and at first met on the second floor at 115 South Main Street. The present church was completed in 1921 and is located on South Sixth Street. Interestingly enough, in the early days in Elkhart, blacks and whites were not segregated, but dined, worshipped, and shopped together. Blacks lived all over the city, several operating businesses along Main Street. It was much later that blacks were separated and concentrated in the area directly south of the railroad tracks. Surprisingly, John S. Weller, an Elkhart newspaperman in 1859, waged an editorial campaign to achieve a then unheard-of goal: to end the segregation of churchgoers by sexes.

Looking north on Main Street south of the corner of Franklin Street in 1884, two years before streetcar tracks were laid. Main Street had not yet been paved. In 1888 Main Street was paved with cedar blocks from north of Jackson to the railroad tracks. Five years later, Jackson was paved with bricks from Main to the Big Four tracks.

Tyler, East Pigeon, Commercial, and Main, from Pigeon to the Main Street bridge, were bricked in 1895, and three years later, the rest of Main Street, from Pigeon to Prairie, was also paved with brick. By 1899 State, Pigeon, High, Franklin, Marion, Harrison, Division, and Second streets were all paved with brick.

In 1888 Main Street, shown here looking south from the corner of Jackson, was just about to be paved with cedar blocks. The streetcar tracks had been laid just two years

before this picture was taken. The banner stretching across the street said "Harrison -Morton," for the Republican Presidential ticket for that election year.

The City Meat Market, in 1888.

The building shown here (in 1877) was originally the home of Joseph Rollins. It was built on the northwest corner of Main and Tyler in 1857, when Tyler was little more than a dirt alley leading to the L.S. & M.S. depot. A man named Jonathan P. Primley worked for Rollins as a druggist. Primley was born in Elkhart in 1852. He married Euphemia Simonton in 1879, three years after establishing his own drug store in this building. In addition to the drug store, he entered the chewing gum business, and in 1892 moved to Chicago, where he merged his California Fruit Chewing Gum business with the American Chicle Company (in 1899). Primley made the first fruit-flavored chewing gum, calling it "Kis-Me." If a girl asked for a stick of "Kis-Me," a fellow could always claim she had said, "Kiss me," and that way one could check to see if the gum was really "Far Better Than A Kiss," as Primley's slogan advertised. Primley never forgot his ties to Elkhart. He gave over $5000 to the Carnegie Library to help get it started. It is interesting to note that the advertisement for Dr. King's Discovery (on the wall) refers to a product made by Herbert E. Bucklen, Sr., which helped build Bucklen's fortune.

The Bucklen Opera House, shortly after it was built in 1884, as seen from the south. The buildings at the left were eventually torn down to make way for the new post office.

Looking south on Main Street from the Clifton House. This picture was taken on February 11, 1886.

RAILROADS

The first attempt to build a railroad through Elkhart County was made in 1835. At that time, no tracks were laid. In 1849 the Northern Indiana Railroad Company was established, but bought by Michigan Southern Railroad later the same year. Then, according to the *Elkhart Truth*, a train consisting of a wood-burning engine, flat cars, and a caboose, puffed its way into Elkhart from White Pigeon, Michigan, on a sunny Friday afternoon in October, 1851.

The Main Street crossing was at its present loca-

The *Robin*, at the roundhouse in Elkhart in 1867. Pictured in the locomotive is W.H. Hall and standing on the ground are (from left to right) A.M. (Gus) Bickel, fireman, and Tom Boyd, engineer. The *Robin* was part of the Michigan Southern and Northern Indiana Railroad Company.

The old L.S. & M.S. depot in 1893. Seven years later, it was torn down and replaced by the present depot in the same location (at the intersection of Second Street and Tyler Avenue).

tion, however, in 1851, a small forest separated the tracks from the village of Elkhart. People from miles around waited up all night by the tracks to see the first "iron horse" arrive. Seven months later, on the 22nd of May, 1852, the first passenger train from Toledo to Chicago came through Elkhart.

In 1869 the Michigan Southern and Northern Indiana line merged with three other railroads to become the Lake Shore and Michigan Southern Railroad. The first roundhouse and repair shops were built about 1867. Most of the L.S.& M.S. shops were completed in 1871. Because of all the shops opening up, there was a great need for railroad workers. The population of Elkhart rose from 1439 in 1860 to 3265 in 1870, and to 6593 in 1880, more than doubling in size each decade. Many men came from Italy to fill the railroad jobs. They settled mostly on the north side of the tracks, along Harrison Street. At about the same time, due to the abundance of jobs, many blacks moved to Elkhart from the South, and settled mostly south of the tracks.

The old L.S.& M.S. line merged with the New York Central Railroad in 1912. As the New York Central continued to grow, so did its employees, finally reaching as many as 2000, making the railroad the largest employer in Elkhart. The number of trains going through Elkhart continued to increase. During, and immediately after, World War II, as many as 124 trains (freight and passenger) travelled over the Main Street

The first railroad YMCA, built in 1884, just east of the old L.S. & M.S. depot on the south side of Tyler Avenue.

The second railroad YMCA, built in 1904, on the north side of Tyler directly west of Second Street (across the street from the present depot).

crossing in one 24-hour period. For a while the average was 109 to 114 trains per day, amounting to an average of nearly five trains per hour all day and all night. All trains stopped in Elkhart, even those that did not stop in larger nearby cities, due to the fact that Elkhart is a railroad division point, and crews change at division points.

As automobiles became plentiful after World War II and air travel increased significantly, the demand for passenger trains dwindled to the point that the service

The Big Four Railroad Station on East Jackson Boulevard, a few yards west of the intersection of Prairie and Jackson, about 1895. Built in 1882, this station was torn down in 1936, after the New York Central Railroad bought out the Big Four.

The observation car of the Twentieth Century Limited, a passenger train, making a stop at the New York Central depot in Elkhart, about 1910.

A typical day at the Elkhart train station, about 1914.

was actually eliminated for a while. The gravity rail classification yard (known as "the hump") was built in 1901. It was upgraded in 1958 to a massive electronic freight classification yard, costing $14 million and utilizing nine analog computers, able to direct as many as 3500 freight cars per day onto 72 classification tracks.

The old Lake Shore and Michigan Southern repair shops.

An aerial view of the round house near Fourth Street, about 1950.

A locomotive and tender in the N.Y.C. roundhouse.

The underpass at "the hump" (the railroad classification yard along West Franklin), west of the city, in 1919, which has since been enlarged and improved. The road going through the underpass is Indiana State Road 19 (or South Nappanee Street). Standing at the edge of the road is Clara Bangerter Norman.

A "modern" New York Central diesel engine.

Luxury service in the dining car of the *Twentieth Century Limited*, "in the good old days."

An aerial view of the Robert Young Electronic Freight Classification Yard, west of the city.

The New York Central Railroad depot, built in 1900, at the intersection of Tyler Avenue and Second Street.

Looking east on Middlebury Street, from the corner of Main and Tyler. The crossing gates are down, holding up traffic, as an eastbound train leaves Elkhart. The Civil War monument can be seen in the left foreground.

LOOKING E
EL

ON MIDDLEBURY ST.

HART IND.

This is a photo of the Exposition of Progress on Main Street in 1926. Looking north from Tyler Avenue, the Bucklen Opera House can be seen at the left. The then new Hotel Elkhart is on the right, a block farther away. The man in the far left foreground plans to celebrate with the large watermelon he is carrying.

In 1884 the Elkhart Water Company built this water tank at what was then the very north end of Main Street, just north of Crawford Street. A fence can be seen in this picture separating the end of Main Street from the Water Company property. At that time, the tank was designed to furnish the necessary water pressure to reach the highest buildings in town. By the turn of the century, better pumps had been installed. The water tank was thought dangerous, and so was torn down. In 1925 the city purchased the Elkhart Water Company for $925,000, and changed its name to the Elkhart City Water Works.

The Johnson Street bridge, shown on the left about 1890, was built in 1887 and replaced in 1918. On the right, the wooden dam across the St. Joseph River is just upstream from where the present dam is located.

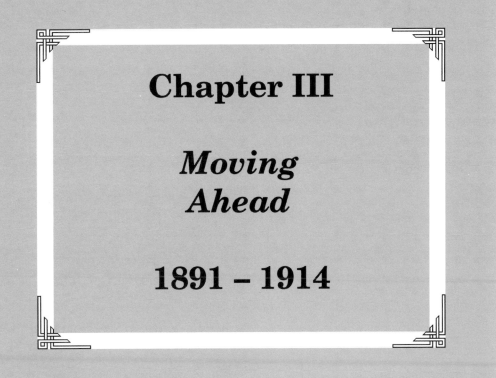

Chapter III

Moving Ahead

1891 – 1914

By the 1890's, the principal means of transportation in Elkhart was the bicycle. There were more than a thousand bicycles in town before the end of the decade. Bicycles were used by policemen on patrol, doctors making house calls, and people making recreational trips to Simonton, Christiana, and Eagle lakes. During this time, there were two bicycle factories in Elkhart, manufacturing Elkhart and Acme bicycles.

It was a time of relative peace for the United States. The Civil War had ended twenty-five years earlier, and the "Great War" (World War I) was yet a long way off. Only in 1898 was this era of military tranquility interrupted, for a few months, as the local boys went off to fight in the Spanish-American War. Their return, before the year's end, was cause for great rejoicing.

Between 1891 and 1914, Miles Medical Company began its growth into a major pharmaceutical business. The C.G. Conn Band Instrument Company became the largest and most important firm of its type in this nation, leading to Elkhart becoming known as the "Band Instrument Capital of the World." There were more than fifty companies producing instruments in Elkhart, including Selmer, Buescher, W.T. Armstrong, Martin, E.K. Blessing, Wurlitzer, Gemeinhardt, Leedy, and Walter Piano (which bought out Conn's piano division). The population increased from 11,360 to more than 21,700, and the first Elkhart High School was built, only to be replaced by a much larger building less than twenty years later.

The YMCA and YWCA were started during this time, and a new City Hall was built on East Franklin Street. It housed the fire and police departments, as well as other city government offices. The post office (on the corner of Main and Jackson) and the Carnegie Library were also erected. E. Hill Turnock returned to Elkhart and began leaving his mark on the architecture of the city. As early as 1899, automobiles began to appear on the streets, and soon more than a dozen companies were manufacturing cars in Elkhart. By 1914 only a few horse-drawn vehicles could be seen on the city's streets.

There were other significant examples of development, and the provision of services to Elkhart's residents. Elkhart General Hospital was established. The police and fire departments became motorized. A new dam over the St. Joseph River was built to provide a greatly needed increase in hydro-electric power. The paving of streets with bricks was begun, because the cedar block paving was deemed unsatisfactory. Many beautiful homes, still standing, were built during these decades. John McNaughton donated McNaughton Park to the city, and the first Chautauqua in Elkhart was held there. New factories, and stores, such as Ziesel's and Drake's, were opened for business. By 1914 most of the major landmarks in Elkhart, as they were to remain for the next forty years, had appeared.

The Memorial Day parade in 1898, seen from the corner of Main and Franklin streets, showing a band and a group called the W. O. W. (Woodmen of the World). In 1978 Midway Motor Lodge replaced all the buildings across the street. The fenced-in yard on the left belonged to the Silas Baldwin residence, and is where Ziesel's was later located. The building on the far right was razed in 1907 and was replaced by the Elks' Temple.

ELKHART POLICE

In 1858 the sole law enforcement officer in Elkhart was the Town Marshal, R. D. Braden, who was elected by the people. While the Marshal usually had five or six policemen working under his supervision in the 1860's, 70's, and 80's, most of them were not full-time employees. The situation changed in 1893, when the metropolitan police commission was organized, in accordance with a new state law.

From 1875 until 1895, the police department was located in the City Hall building on the northeast corner of High and Second streets. In 1895 it was moved to the new City Hall building on East Franklin Street. By 1898 there were ten policemen on the force, and by 1914, there were nineteen, including two plain clothesmen (detectives). The Elkhart Police Department became motorized about 1910.

R. D. Braden, Elkhart's first Town Marshal came here in 1844. He was also the first millwright in Elkhart, doing all the work on the old Beardsley flour mill.

A picture of the police department ambulance in front of Elkhart General Hospital, about 1914. The driver is Jack Northrop.

Three Elkhart police officers have been killed in the line of duty:

Willard Burton	1888
Oran Shelmadine	1920
Henry Wentz	1924

The entire Elkhart Police Department, in 1914, outside police headquarters on East Franklin Street. William H. Roth was Chief of Police at that time.

BUCKLEN

Herbert E. Bucklen.

Bucklen Opera House, Elkhart, Ind.

Herbert E. Bucklen, born in New York in 1848, came to Elkhart as a young boy. He started one of the first soda fountains in northern Indiana in his father's drug store, on the northeast corner of Main and Jackson. After successfully developing a number of patented medicines, he began to invest in real estate, eventually owning many buildings and acres of land in Elkhart and Chicago. Perhaps he is best remembered for making the massive renovation of Clifton House, renamed the Hotel Bucklen, and for the Bucklen Opera House. Bucklen moved to Chicago in 1885, but kept in contact with Elkhart. When he died in 1917, he was buried in "God's Half Acre," a private cemetery located on the family farm, on Redfield Road in Cass County, Michigan.

The Bucklen Opera House, built in 1884 on the northwest corner of Main and Harrison streets, had a seating capacity of 1,200, and was the scene of many memorable events. In addition to featuring such famous stars as Houdini and singer Jenny Lind (the Swedish nightingale), the Opera House was frequently used by dramatic, vaudeville, and musical traveling groups as a last stop performance before opening in Chicago, giving Elkhartans "sneak previews." The great Creatore and John Philip Sousa brought their bands to perform here. High school graduation ceremonies were also held here for a number of years. The first motion picture in Elkhart was shown at the Bucklen in 1896, the admission charge being five cents for seats in the balcony and ten cents for seats on the main floor. The Opera House eventually became known as the Bucklen Theater, and was one of Elkhart's four movie theaters during the 1940's and 1950's. The last time a movie was shown at the Bucklen Theater was in the fall of 1956. Spacious second floor rooms housed a ballet school for many years (the Academy of Ballet Arts, and later, the Warren School of Ballet). A large third floor room was used as a rehearsal hall by the Elkhart Symphony Orchestra. After some alterations, various stores occupied what had been the seating area of the theater. Due to years of neglect and fear that the building would collapse, it was torn down in 1986.

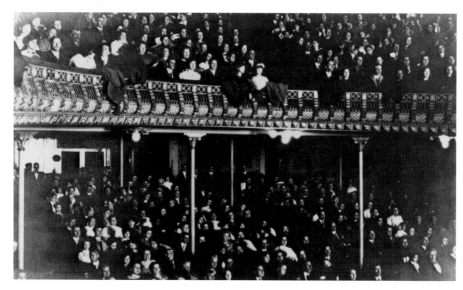

The interior of the Bucklen Opera House was often filled to capacity for concerts and performances around the turn of the century.

Clifton House (the second hotel of that name to occupy this location) was built in 1863 on the southeast corner of Main and Jackson by J. R. Beardsley, B. L. Davenport and Silas Baldwin. At that time, Main Street was not yet paved, and stagecoaches made regular stops in Elkhart, as shown in this picture.

The Hotel Bucklen, which is actually the same building as the Clifton House, opened in 1889, after major renovations. It had many luxury features, such as private and public baths, elevators, and a fine dining room. Later it was badly damaged by a fire. It was remodeled in 1958, once again named Clifton House (in 1960), and operated as a hotel until another fire, in 1969, finally ended the use of the building once and for all. It was razed in 1973.

"Ruthmere," the residence of Albert R. and Elizabeth Baldwin Beardsley, was built in 1908 at 302 East Beardsley Avenue. It was named after their only child, Ruth, who died in infancy in the 1880's. Ruthmere was designed by E. Hill Turnock, and opened to the public as a museum in 1973, after being restored by Robert Beardsley.

The home of Andrew Hubbell Beardsley, at 226 East Beardsley Avenue, next door to Ruthmere on the west, was built in 1908. It was designed by E. Hill Turnock, and was torn down in 1964 to make way for the new Presbyterian Church parking lot.

The Benjamin L. and Sarah Davenport home, built in 1850 and torn down in 1941, was located on the northeast corner of Main Street and East Beardsley Avenue, now the site of the Russell Warner home. Mrs. Davenport was the daughter of Havilah Beardsley.

Located on the northwest corner of Prospect and Bower streets is the former home of Mrs. Chauncey Baldwin, built in 1907.

The home of Philo Morehous was built in 1849 on the east side of North Main Street, between Jefferson and Jackson. Occupied by the Elks Lodge in its later years, it was demolished in 1960 to make room for the McDonald's parking lot.

St. Joseph Manor, an early "subdivision" of Elkhart, north of East Jackson Boulevard, about 1919. The second house from the left is the Heinheis home. It was designed by E. Hill Turnock for the W. H. Foster family in 1917. (Foster was mayor of Elkhart in 1918.) Turnock also designed the other homes in this picture.

The Compton home on the north side of Jefferson Street, between Second and Third, was designed by E. Hill Turnock to be a "double house" (duplex). In 1904 Herman Compton and his bride, Grace, moved into half of this home. Herman's parents, George and Lizzie Compton, lived in the other half. Later this house was turned into the Jefferson Apartments.

This home was built on the northwest corner of Second and Lexington in 1893, for Col. Tucker. It was the William B. Pratt home for about 20 years, and then became the Charles S. Drake home from about 1920 to 1926. After that, it was the White Funeral Home, until it was torn down about 1947, to make way for the new General Telephone Company building. The buckeye tree in the yard, a source of treasured souvenirs for local boys, was taken out along with the house.

The Winchester mansion, designed by E. Hill Turnock, was built on the northwest corner of Second and Harrison in 1905. Charles H. Winchester was president of First National Bank, from 1887 until his death in 1917. At the time Mr. and Mrs. Winchester moved into this home, their daughter and son-in-law, Nellie and William H. Knickerbocker, moved in with them. Knickerbocker started as cashier at the bank in 1886 and became president in 1917, after the death of his father-in-law. After her husband died in 1937, Mrs. Knickerbocker lived in the mansion until her death in 1947. Mr. & Mrs. Knickerbocker are shown here sitting in their car in front of the home.

The Carl D. Greenleaf home, built in 1917 at 1415 Greenleaf Boulevard, two years after Greenleaf bought the C. G. Conn Band Instrument Company and the *Elkhart Truth*.

Still located on the southwest corner of Second and Jefferson, the James Cornish home was built in 1871. This picture, taken about 1885, shows Wilmet (Millie), Jennie, and Mr. Cornish in the yard. Mrs. Cornish is on the porch. The Cornish family's horse and carriage are waiting on Jefferson Street, beside the home.

The house shown at the left is still on the southwest corner of Lexington and Fourth. The other two homes are also still standing. This picture was taken about 1900.

The Henry C. Dodge home was built about 1885, on the southwest corner of Second and Marion, and torn down in 1924. By the time this picture was taken, it had become the Stephens and Son Funeral Home. In the right foreground, can be seen the horse-drawn hearse of Stephens and Son. In 1928 A. G. Zelle purchased the business, after Henry Stephen's death. When Lloyd Hartzler became his partner in 1948, the name of the funeral home was changed to Zelle-Hartzler Funeral Home. Zelle retired in 1951, and Tom Gutermuth became a partner in 1955. The name was changed one more time to Hartzler-Gutermuth Funeral Home. It is now located in the former home of Dr. Franklin Miles, on the southwest corner of Franklin and Fourth.

R. W. Monger once lived in this home, on the southeast corner of Franklin and Fifth streets, across from Central Christian Church. This picture was taken about 1910.

Once the residence of G. W. Frederick, at 1129 Prairie Street, this is now the Westbrook-Metz Funeral Home. The car in front is a 1910 Buick.

This picture, taken about 1900, shows the L. Helfrich & Son Furniture store, located at 506-508 South Main Street, in the I.O.O.F. (International Order of the Odd Fellows) building.

The northwest corner of Main and High, about 1900. The building on the far left is H. B. Sykes & Company dry goods store, later Drake's department store.

A camel caravan in Elkhart? No, only a procession from a Buffalo Bill Wild West show. The camels are heading south on Second Street, in front of the old Central School, in 1909.

The Elkhart Railroad Centennial parade on October 5, 1951. In the left foreground is the A & P grocery store, located in the old Armory building at the northeast corner of Main and Jefferson streets. Just beyond the A & P is the old Philo Morehous home (at that time the Elks Lodge). The Bucklen Hotel can be seen in the distance.

PARADES....

Looking south on Main Street from Jackson, during the Women's Civic League parade in 1915.

The Ringling Brothers Circus parade in 1898, looking east on Pigeon Street (Lexington) from the intersection with Vistula. The first Elkhart High School (later Samuel Strong School) is in the center behind the elephants. The spire of the new St. John's Episcopal Church can be seen in the background on the right. The parade is heading toward the circus grounds at Johnson Commons, west of the bridge.

The Mason Parade on May 18, 1911, looking south on Main Street from the corner of High. The building on the right is the old Kavanagh and Pollard grocery store, presently the site of Ameritrust National Bank. All the buildings on the left have been demolished, making way for the Midway Motor Lodge. The barrel-shaped vehicle, in the foreground, was used to spray water on dirt streets to keep down the dust.

Looking north on Main Street, from the corner of High Street, during the Industrial Parade on September 25, 1913. The three story building in the left foreground was the H. B. Sykes dry goods store, later Drake's department store.

An advertising float, for the Industrial Parade of 1913, waits to take its place in the formation.

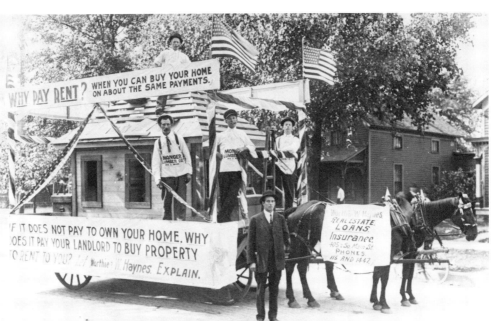

This is a picture of the Indiana and Michigan Electric Company float, in front of the electric company building at 112 West Lexington Avenue, waiting to join the Industrial Parade, on September 25, 1913.

HOSPITALS

Elkhart General Hospital had its beginning at a public meeting in the First Congregational Church, on October 6, 1908. A committee was formed to draw up organizational plans. The General Hospital association was incorporated in 1909. The following year, Dr. Franklin Miles offered to donate $10,000 to the hospital fund, if $30,000 could be raised from other sources. By early 1911, the fund-raising campaign had received $47,000 in pledges. Later that year, a site near McNaughton Park was selected, and construction began in 1912, being completed in August of 1913. The original building was designed by E. Hill Turnock. Since then, Elkhart General Hospital has undergone so much growth, that the original part can hardly be seen.

The direct predecessor of Elkhart General was Clark Hospital, located at 126 North Clark Street. This hospital's property was willed in trust to a citizens' committee by Mrs. Hannah Whiting Clark. She and her husband, James E. Clark, came to Elkhart in 1845. He died in 1863, and she in 1900. Clark Homeopathic Hospital had opened in 1899, the staff consisting of all the physicians in town and nine nurses. With a patient capacity of seventeen, Clark Hospital took care of 300 patients during the year of 1909. The Clark Hospital property was converted into $3315, for the Elkhart General Hospital fund in 1912.

The original Elkhart General Hospital, about 1914. It was designed by E. Hill Turnock. The Elkhart Police Department ambulance is shown by the front door of the building.

A patient's room at Elkhart General Hospital, about 1914.

The X-Ray laboratory at Elkhart General Hospital, about 1915.

The Nurses' Home, built to house the nurses at Elkhart General Hospital, about 1914.

A picture of the nurses of Elkhart General, about 1915.

Elkhart General Hospital in 1989, after undergoing many expansions.

Clark Hospital, about 1905, located on Clark Street. The building later became an apartment house.

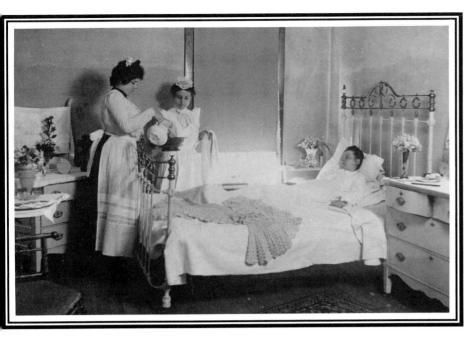

A patient being cared for by two nurses at Clark Hospital.

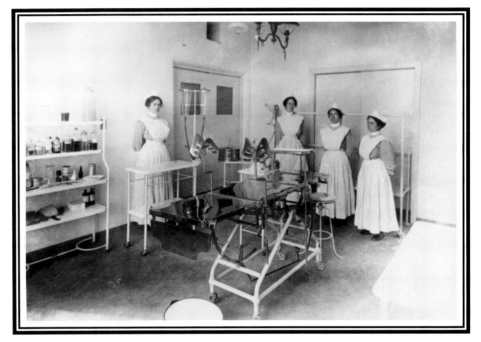

The delivery room, at Clark Hospital, between 1905 and 1914.

Dr. Crow's Osteopathic Home, on the southwest corner of Second and Franklin, about 1905. The building is still located there, minus the porches.

ST. JOSEPH RIVER DAM

The very first dam in Elkhart was across Christiana Creek, constructed by George Crawford and John Huntsman in 1829 to provide power for their grist mill. Three years later, Abner Simonton built a dam across the Elkhart River. The first dam across the St. Joseph River was built by the Elkhart Hydraulic Company in 1867-68 at a cost of $100,000. Most of the names of the nine men involved in this venture are still familiar in Elkhart today. They were John Davenport, John McNaughton, Samuel Hoke, James R. Beardsley, B. L. Davenport, William Proctor, Dr. A. S. Davenport, A. P. Simonton, and Samuel S. Strong.

Dams of this period were all made in a similar fashion. Trees were uprooted by teams of horses or oxen and dragged to the river. There they were placed parallel to the current, with roots downstream and trunks (stripped of branches) pointing upstream. Then, to keep the trees in place as the current pushed against the root ends, sand, gravel, and rocks were used to weigh the trunks down and fill in the spaces between them. This type of dam required frequent repair due

The first dam over the St. Joseph River, looking downstream (west). This picture was taken about 1868.

This is how the St. Joseph River dam looked about 1910.

to the effects of weather, flooding, and gradual erosion.

When the demand for hydraulic power exceeded the capabilities of the dam, flashboards were added to increase the water level by at least three feet. The flashboards gave way from time to time and needed replacing. By 1910 it had become obvious that a better, higher dam was needed, one that could regulate the amount of water flow. So, in 1911, work began on a reinforced concrete dam just downstream from the original one. The new dam was completed in 1912, and is still in operation today.

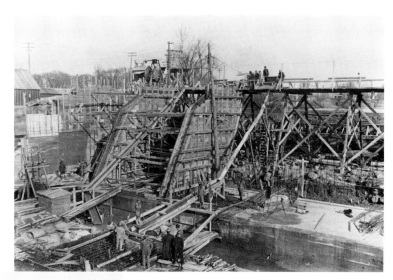

The new St. Joseph River dam, under construction in 1911.

The new dam nearing completion, in 1912.

The new hydro-electric generating plant, at the south end of the newly constructed dam, in 1913. The bridge on the right spanned a canal, which carried water to factories located between Elkhart Avenue and the river, prior to the building of the new dam.

MAIN STREET BRIDGE

From the beginning, the location of Elkhart was blessed by having three streams (the St. Joseph and Elkhart rivers, and Christiana Creek) flow through it, providing beauty, hydraulic power, and a natural "highway" for transportation and commerce. However, there was a drawback to this blessing. Some means of crossing the St. Joseph River was needed to connect Pulaski and other settlers on the north side, to the Elkhart business and residential areas on the south side.

The first solution came from Dr. Havilah Beardsley, who lived on the north side of the river and owned a great deal of land on the south side. He petitioned the government, and received permission to establish a rope ferry across the river. This arrangement consisted of a rope connected from a tree on one side of the river to a tree on the other side. A hook attached to

the rope, was secured to the ferry by another rope. Then, the ferry was poled across the river, by using a long pole that reached the bottom of the river, propelling the ferry forward. The rope and hook arrangement kept the ferry from being swept downstream by the swift current.

Obviously a better method was needed. So, in 1837, John Proctor built a wooden bridge across the St. Joseph River, at the location of the present Main Street bridge. It was intended to be a covered bridge, but that was never done. This bridge, however, served well until the spring of 1844, when the first steamboat appeared.

From 1830 until 1844, many arks (cumbersome vessels resembling scows or large rafts) and keel boats had carried a variety of cargos to and from Elkhart, and various Great Lakes ports. Warehouses had been built along the Elkhart River, from its mouth by Island Park, as far upstream as General William B. Mitchell's warehouse at the east end of Marion Street.

The second wooden Main Street bridge. Havilah Beardsley's home (built in 1848) is in the center background. An east wing to the house was added later.

The third Main Street bridge, looking west. In the distance can be seen the piers and railings of the old (second) wooden bridge. Just to the right of the middle of the bridge, the old Beardsley flour mill can be seen. The Beardsley paper mill is visible, just to the left of the center of the bridge.

When the first steamboat arrived, it could not get past the wooden bridge and proceed up the Elkhart River, because the smokestack was too tall to go under the bridge. The steamboat was tied to the bridge overnight to allow time for a solution to be worked out. The solution consisted of removing the timbers of the middle span of the bridge, allowing the steamboat to pass. Everyone agreed that this could not be done every time a steamboat came upstream, so hinges were added to the steamboat stacks. Then, at the cry of "Low bridge, lower the stack," the necessary adjustment could easily be made. The arrival of the first train in 1851, south of the village through the woods, signalled the beginning of the end for steamboats in Elkhart.

About a year later, the first wooden bridge was carried away by the current, because the timbers had rotted out. By this time, a dispute had arisen between the merchants on Main Street and those on Second Street as to which of their streets would become the major thoroughfare in the future. A compromise resulted. The second wooden bridge was built halfway between Main and Second, and was reached from Water Street (later Pottowattomi Drive). This bridge was in place from about 1853 until 1871.

In 1871 an arched iron bridge was built in the original location of the Main Street bridge, the controversy having been settled. When this bridge was dismantled in 1891, one of the two spans was taken to become the first good bridge to Island Park. The other span was taken elsewhere in the county. That same year, a new steel truss bridge (the fourth Main Street bridge) was erected. It lasted 36 years, until it was replaced by the present concrete bridge in 1927.

The fourth Main Street bridge, looking west from Island Park.

The third Main Street bridge, looking north. The boy on the left is Frank Brown. The Elkhart Water Company water tank can be seen in the distance, a block or two north of the bridge.

The fifth (and present) Main Street bridge. When this bridge was built, the streetcar tracks crossed the bridge from West Beardsley Avenue, which was still paved with bricks.

C. G. CONN

For many years, Elkhart was known as the "Band Instrument Capital of the World." This was due, in no small part, to the efforts of Charles Gerard Conn. Born in 1844 in the state of New York, he moved with his parents, Charles J. and Sara Benjamin Conn, to Three Rivers, Michigan, in 1850 and to Elkhart in 1851.

At age 17, Gerard (as he liked to be called) joined the Union Army to fight in the Civil War where he advanced from the rank of private to captain, and helped drive Morgan's Raiders out of Indiana. He was captured and tried to escape three times, but was not successful.

Upon his return to Elkhart at the end of the Civil War, Conn entered the grocery and bakery business. He also continued playing the cornet, which he had learned to play at an early age. He married Kate Hazeleton, a local girl, and in 1874 they had a daughter, Sallie.

In 1873 an event occurred which changed Conn's life, and the course of history in Elkhart. He became involved in a brawl which left him with a badly cut lip. After the lip healed, the scar that remained made it nearly impossible for him to play his cornet. To overcome this problem, Conn made a special mouthpiece cushion out of rubber. This not only allowed him to play his own horn again, but also drew the attention of every horn player who saw it. Since most of them wanted one for themselves, Conn decided to go into business making rubber-cushioned mouthpieces.

In 1875 Conn moved his business across Jackson Boulevard to a building behind the brick post office. In June of that year, a French musical instrument maker named DuPont

The first C. G. Conn factory, near the corner of Jackson Boulevard and Elkhart Avenue, operated in this building from 1877 until it burned down in 1883.

The C. G. Conn factory, designed by E. Hill Turnock and located at 1101 East Beardsley Avenue, was operating soon after the second factory burned down, in 1910.

stopped to see Conn and asked permission to use some of his equipment, to repair several horns. After watching DuPont for a few days, Conn felt sure that he could make a horn himself. Later that year he did just that, producing the first cornet made in America. In less than a year, three European craftsmen had been brought to Elkhart, to help Conn build band instruments.

By 1877 the variety of operations and the volume of business required larger facilities. Conn bought a three story building near the corner of East Jackson Boulevard and Elkhart Avenue. Situated on the Elkhart River, it was operated by hydraulic power alone. By 1880 there were more than 80 employees, and in addition to the cornet, other instruments were being made. Then, on the night of Conn's 39th birthday, January 29, 1883, a fire broke out in the packing room of the factory. It spread quickly and consumed the whole building, despite the best efforts of the fire department.

Colonel C. G. Conn in Civil War uniform.

Samuel Strong built this house in the 700 block of Strong Avenue in 1884. It was later purchased by C. G. Conn, and is still standing today.

This house, known as the Conn mansion and located in the 700 block of Strong Avenue, is the one that belonged to Samuel Strong. It was extensively renovated by C. G. Conn after he bought it. His wife, Kate, lived in it until her death, in 1924.

Lawndale, C. G. Conn's "country home," was located on the property at the southeast corner of Osolo Road and East Bristol Street.

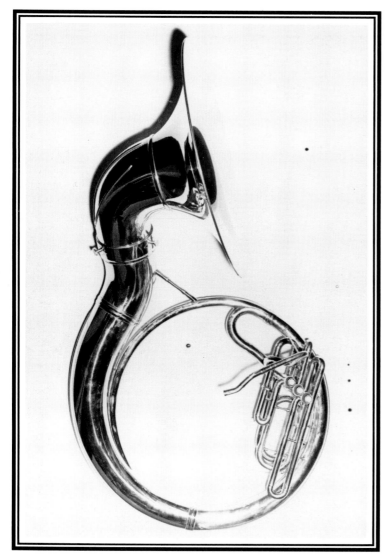

With no city water works system, the firefighters had to bore through 18 inches of ice in the Elkhart River, to get sufficient water to fight the fire. Conn was not easily daunted, however, and soon had a larger building built on the same site.

Not satisfied with being just a businessman, C. G. Conn was active in politics and publishing as well. In 1880 he was elected mayor of Elkhart and served in that post for four years. He was elected to the Indiana General Assembly in 1888, and in 1892 was elected to the United States House of Representatives.

In 1889 Conn bought the mechanical equipment of the *Elkhart Review* and started his own newspaper, which he called the *Elkhart Truth.* Its first issue was published on October 15, 1889. He held the position of editor until he went to Washington in 1893 to serve one term in Congress. While in Washington, he purchased the *Washington Times,* and operated that newspaper for the two years he was a congressman. He sold the *Times* before returning to Elkhart.

Meanwhile, the Conn band instrument company continued to expand. In 1889 it produced the first American saxophone and the first all-metal clarinet, followed by the first double bell euphonium the next year. A branch plant was opened in Massachusetts in 1887, and by 1893 the company was employing more than 300 workers, including additional skilled craftsmen brought over from Europe.

The Sousaphone, which is the largest and lowest pitched of the brass instruments, was built in a circular form, making it easier to carry in marching bands. It has a large bore, giving a deep, rich, organ-like tone, and has a bell that faces out (rather than up like a tuba) to aid in projecting the sound.

Mr. Ted Pounder, inventor of the Sousaphone, is shown here working on one of the giant horns. He was employed by Conn's for many years. This picture was taken about 1950.

70

Many celebrated musicians and band directors used and endorsed Conn instruments, including Patrick Gilmore (known as the Father of American Brass Bands), Liberati, Herbert L. Clarke (considered to be the greatest cornetist of his time), and the great Creatore. When John Philip Sousa took his band on a world tour, Conn gave each member of the band a jeweled, engraved Conn instrument. In 1898 the Conn company introduced a brand new instrument, the Sousaphone, following Sousa's specifications.

C. G. Conn had many enemies, some due to his muckraking days as editor of the *Elkhart Truth*, and some reportedly due to his interest in women other than his wife. He also had other troubles. In 1910 fire completely destroyed the Conn factory a second time. Once again he built an even grander, larger building (designed by E. Hill Turnock) in just a few months, this time at a new location at 1101 East Beardsley Avenue. Due to a shortage of funds, Conn decided to sell the factory and the newspaper to C. D. Greenleaf in 1915. He then moved permanently to California, without his wife and daughter. He divorced his wife, married Suzanne Cohn, and at age 70, fathered a son. Conn died in 1931 in California at the age of 86, too poor to pay for his own funeral. The Elkhart Masonic Lodge brought his body back to be buried in Grace Lawn Cemetery.

This E flat bass is just one of the many "Wonder" horn models made by the C. G. Conn Band Instrument Company.

The polishing room at the C. G. Conn factory on East Beardsley Avenue, in 1943. George Adams, at far right, worked for Conn's for 46 years.

This is what Main Street looked like in 1914. The buildings at the left have been replaced with the present Ameritrust National Bank. The *Elkhart Truth* building can be seen at the right, and in the distance, the Hotel Bucklen.

73

CITY HALL

Henry C. Wright, Elkhart's first mayor, was defeated in his bid for re-election by James R. Beardsley, son of Havilah.

When did Elkhart really begin? The 1924 centennial celebration was held to honor the naming of Christiana Creek 100 years earlier. In 1832 the first plat of Elkhart was laid out. The centennial celebration in 1958 commemorated Elkhart becoming a town, an increase in size and status over being just a village. But in 1875, Elkhart reached the lofty classification of a city. At this time, Elkhart's population was about 6500. The vote in favor of city government was 575 to 561. This required a number of changes, among them the need to elect a mayor and city council, and to build a city hall to house the new elements of government. Henry C. Wright was elected first mayor of Elkhart on May 11, 1875, defeating John McNaughton.

The first city hall was built in 1875, on the northeast corner of Second and High streets, facing south on High. The first floor of the three story building was used by the fire department, and housed the city jail. The second floor provided room for offices, such as city clerk and treasurer, and for the city council chamber. The third floor was used for public meetings and dances. However, the ringing of the fire bell on top of the building caused such vibrations, that use of the third floor was discontinued, after a few years, for fear that the building would collapse.

In 1895 a new structure was built, on the south side of East Franklin, to house the police and fire departments, and to provide temporary quarters for city clerk, treasurer, judge, and council chamber. These "temporary" quarters were used for twenty years until the current municipal building was built in 1916, on the northwest corner of Second and High, at a cost of $100,000. The original city hall was torn down about 1900, and replaced by the new Carnegie Library, in 1903.

Elkhart's first city hall, located on the northeast corner of Second and High, from 1875 to 1900.

Long known as the police and fire department building, this structure (still standing on East Franklin Street) was also Elkhart's city hall, from 1895 until 1916.

The Municipal Building, designed by E. Hill Turnock, was built on the northwest corner of Second and High in 1916, and has served as city hall ever since. This is the same corner where the old "Shot Tower" was built, in 1835.

THE CORNER OF SECOND AND HIGH

SECOND STREET, ELKHART, IND.

Looking south, about 1913, the buildings from left to right are: the Carnegie Library, the domed Presbyterian Church, the corner of the Monger Building, the steeple of Trinity Methodist Church, and Elkhart High School. Everything in this picture is gone now, even the trees. And Second Street has been completely re-paved.

Looking northwest, from the top of the old Miles Building, in 1907, work is just being finished on the Monger Building. The Trinity Methodist Church rectory is to the left of the church. Behind it, in the distance, can be seen the footings for the new Central School. To the right of Trinity Methodist is the old Central School, built in 1868. Its Annex, built in 1884, is behind it (to the left, directly behind the church, in this picture). To the right of the school is the "Shot Tower," on the northwest corner of Second and High, almost completely hidden by trees that lined both streets. At the far right, is the old steepled, brick Presbyterian Church. The other two buildings (in the right foreground) housed commercial and residential units, including Lloyd's grocery store (on the northeast corner of Second and Franklin). In the distant background can be seen the roof of Samuel Strong School (then Elkhart High School), and the steeples of First Baptist and St. John's Episcopal churches.

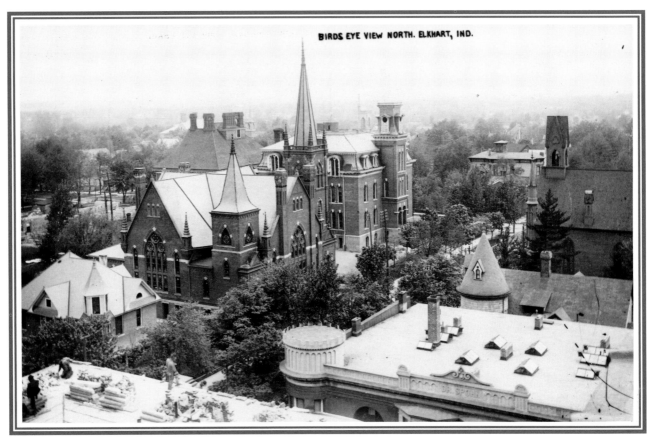

BIRDS EYE VIEW NORTH, ELKHART, IND.

Long the center of culture, education, religion, and government in Elkhart, the area around the corner of Second and High streets has undergone a number of changes over the years. Today it is still a significant area, with the new Elkhart Public Library on the south-east corner, the Municipal Building on the northwest corner, and the parking lot of the county courts building on the southwest corner. An Ameritrust National Bank parking lot occupies the northeast corner.

Several changes can be seen from 1907 to 1914, when this picture was taken from the top of the old Miles Building. A corner of the completed Monger Building appears in the far left foreground. Old Central School and its Annex have been demolished, and replaced by the new Elkhart High School. To the right of the school is a cleared lot, where the "Shot Tower" had stood since 1835, but which was soon to be the site of the new Municipal Building, on the northwest corner of Second and High. At the far right is the domed Presbyterian Church, which replaced the steepled one.

In 1922 the Elkhart Plan Commission envisioned this layout for the area around the corner of Second and High. In it the Masonic Temple, the YWCA building, the Municipal Building, St. John's Episcopal Church, and Samuel Strong School would all have been left where they are today. Also left would have been the Christian Science, domed Presbyterian, Trinity Methodist, and First Baptist churches (all of which have been torn down). The Carnegie Library would have had an extension added on the north side, blocking off the alley. The Elkhart High School auditorium would have been added in a different location, with an entrance on Third Street instead of on High. Room for further expansion for Elkhart High School was provided along Franklin, all the way up to Second Street. The block bounded by Second, Lexington, Third, and High streets would have been turned into a central park, with a band stand in the middle, and the Municipal Building in one corner. A hotel was planned for the northeast corner of Second and Lexington, and a Community Building, with tennis courts, placed along the north side of Lexington, between Second and Third, where the Telephone Company is now located.

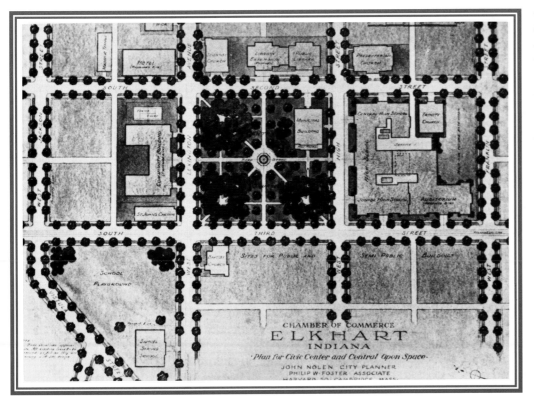

77

FIELDHOUSE

The Fieldhouse story in this area began in 1837, when Ira G. Hubbard walked from Detroit to Elkhart, in search of a homestead. Finding what he was looking for four miles southwest of Elkhart, he built a log cabin and brought his wife, Catherine, and their three year old son, Andrew, to this area (in a covered wagon). Hubbard purchased a total of 154 acres, on which he built a home for his family, in 1849, to replace the log cabin. A daughter, Mary, was born on the farm in 1851.

Two years earlier, John W. Fieldhouse was born on a farm near White Pigeon, Michigan. His father, William Fieldhouse, had been born in Acomb, York, England, in 1812, and had come to the White Pigeon area in 1832. There he met and married Hannah Barker, who had come from the same town in England, but had never met William until after she arrived in White Pigeon. They had seven children, of which John was the youngest.

In 1868 John's brother, Edward, opened a meat market in Elkhart, at 121 West Jackson Boulevard, and two years later, John joined him. When Edward died in 1873, John continued operating the meat market for another ten years. He then sold that business to a childhood friend, and opened a real estate office at 111 West Pigeon Street (now Lexington Avenue). John married Mary J. Hubbard, and they lived in a house he had built at 209 South Second Street. In 1892 he built another house for his family, next door, on the southwest corner of Second and Lexington. It was a beautiful landmark in downtown Elkhart, until it was

Ira G. and
Catherine Hubbard

The Hubbard Hill homestead. Standing in front of the house (from left to right) are Mary J. Fieldhouse, John W. Fieldhouse, and their son, Charlie. This house is still standing on the west side of Indiana 19 South, at the turn-off to Jimtown.

torn down in 1964, to make way for the new Indiana and Michigan Electric Company.

John Fieldhouse was a prominent citizen in Elkhart for many years. He was in the real estate business for 55 years, vice-president, president, and then chairman of the board of St. Joseph Valley Bank for over 35 years, served on both the city council and the county commission, and was agent for H. E. Bucklen for many years, eventually buying many pieces of property from the Bucklen estate. When John W. Fieldhouse died in 1938, his estate included about 300 dwelling houses, 250 vacant lots, eight factory plants, ten store buildings, the Bucklen Hotel and Bucklen Theater, as well as the Lerner Theater.

John and Mary Fieldhouse had two daughters and one son. Their son, Charles Hubbard Fieldhouse, joined his father's real estate business in 1901, and continued in it throughout his life. Charlie used to

continued on page 80

John W. and Mary J. Fieldhouse, about 1910.

To the left of Kibbe's drug store is John Fieldhouse's meat market, located at 121 West Jackson Boulevard. His meat delivery wagon is standing in front of the market. This picture was taken between 1873 and 1883. In a room above Kibbe's drug store, C. G. Conn first started making mouthpieces and band instruments. He made his first cornet there in 1875.

The Fieldhouse home, built in 1892, on the southwest corner of Second and Lexington. Mr. and Mrs. John Fieldhouse and their son, Charlie, are sitting in the buggy. This picture was taken in 1904. Their first home, which can be seen at the left, is still standing.

enjoy saying, "My main reason for staying in business is just to see what will happen next." He and his wife, Alma, lived in the house at the corner of Second and Lexington for many years. People walking by the house could always tell when spring had arrived, by the crocuses growing in the front lawn.

Charlie Fieldhouse turned the old Hubbard homestead, on Indiana 19 South, into a museum housing all his antiques, old cars, and mementos collected over the years. After his death in 1969 (Alma had died in 1968.), the Hubbard property was sold to the North Central District of the Missionary Church, and turned into a retirement center. The items in the museum were sold at auction.

Charlie Fieldhouse was also a prominent citizen of Elkhart for many years. His contributions include the development of the High Dive swimming area, the establishment of the Hubbard Hill Museum, and the publication of his interesting book, *For Land Sakes — 73 Years in Real Estate*. In his book he tells of one tenant, C. J. Warnke, who in 1932, in a rental building at 515 Baldwin Street, invented the fluorescent electric light, and then sold the patent to General Electric.

Behind the fire chief's car is the Fieldhouse real estate office, at 111 West Lexington Avenue, built in 1883.

Charles H. Fieldhouse, about 1957.

The Fieldhouse office in 1904. The office, inside and out, looked much the same at the time of Charlie's death, as it does in this picture.

80

NEWSPAPERS

In the early days, as in most of the nation, newspapers in Elkhart tended to be highly politically-oriented and short-lived. Once the political battle, which caused a newspaper to begin publishing, was fought and won or lost, the reason for that newspaper's existence usually ended — and so did the newspaper. Competition with other newspapers caused some to cease for financial reasons. The first newspaper in Elkhart was named the *Elkhart Advertiser,* a weekly that began in 1844, and lasted less than two years. In 1855 another weekly, the *Elkhart Herald*, was begun, but it also lasted no more than two years.

The *Elkhart Weekly Review* was started in 1859 and continued until 1910. Thirteen years later, the *Daily Review* was added, by the same publishers, and continued until 1920, at which time it was bought out by its arch rival, the *Elkhart Truth.* From 1844 to date, there have been at least eighteen different newspapers in Elkhart. Some, like the *Elkhart Progressive Democrat* (in 1914) and the *Elkhart Daily News* (in 1924), lasted only two or three months. The *Democratic Union* was started in 1867, and continued until 1890. It, too, was purchased by the *Truth.* During the time of its publication, its name was changed four times — first to the *Democrat,* then to the *Elkhart Monitor,* next to the *Democratic Sentinel,* and finally to the *Daily Sentinel.* Some other newspapers in the city were: the *Elkhart Weekly Observer* (in 1872), the *Elkhart Gazeteer* (a monthly publication starting in 1868), the *Elkhart Journal* (in 1880), and the *Elkhart Independent* (in 1884).

Since 1920 there has been only one newspaper in town, the *Elkhart Truth.* It was founded on October 15, 1889, by Col. C. G. Conn, and was published in the mornings for the first four months, and then published in the evenings. A Sunday edition was soon abandoned, but a weekly edition (published along with the daily edition) continued into the early 1900's. For its first two years, the *Truth* was published in the Blackburn Block (at 405-407 South Main Street). It was moved to a building at 308 South Main in 1891, and to 416 South Second in 1918. Forty-seven years later, all operations were moved, one more time, across the street to the Equity Building (now Communicana).

Conn sold his interest in the *Elkhart Truth* to C. D. Greenleaf and A. H. Beardsley in 1915. At that time, a weekly subscription cost only ten cents. Circulation in 1916 was 3906; in 1920, 9352; and in 1940, 15,346. Tom Keene joined the *Truth* staff in 1911, and became editor in 1915. He retired in 1952, and was succeeded as editor by John F. Dille, Jr.

This is a picture of the *Elkhart Truth* Publishing Company, which was located at 416 South Second Street, from 1918 until 1965.

Reproduced here are nameplates of some of the newspapers which at one time were published in Elkhart.

MILES

Franklin Lawrence Miles first came to Elkhart about 1860, as a young boy. His early schooling, in the East, was followed by earning a law degree through studies at Yale and Columbia, and a medical degree, after preparation at the University of Michigan and Rush Medical College (in Chicago). By the time he earned his M.D., he was 28 years old. He married a fellow medical student, Ellen Lighthall. Dr. Miles opened his first office in their home on Franklin Street. Even though he specialized in eye and ear problems, he treated a wide variety of illnesses, some of them apparently caused by contaminated water and other unsanitary conditions, in Elkhart, at that time.

An advertisement, in the *Elkhart City Directory of 1877,* stated that F. Lawrence Miles, M.D., maintained an office in the Morehous Block on the northeast corner of Main and Jackson, with office hours from 1 to 4 p.m. He was described as "Physician, Oculist and Aurist." At this time, his wife, Ellen, now also a physician, shared his office. After they had been married eight years, they both contracted "typho-malaria" and went to Christiana Lake to recuperate. Franklin recovered, but Ellen died, leaving him with two young daughters and a son.

Shortly after this, Dr. Miles developed what became one of his most famous medical products,

Dr. Franklin L. Miles, founder of Miles Laboratories.

The home of Dr. Miles, located on the southwest corner of Franklin and Fourth streets, is now the Hartzler-Gutermuth Funeral Home.

Nervine. He believed that when nerves were unhealthy or strained, the whole body was disturbed. Along with distributing his new medicine, he published journals which advertised his products and educated the public, showing how nerves worked, and what effect they had on the body. He also discussed how sensible living could minimize disease.

In 1885, with the help of two partners, Dr. Miles incorporated his business of producing medicine. These two partners were replaced two years later by George Compton, an Elkhart drygoods merchant, and A. R. Burns, a local druggist. Then, in 1889, Albert R. Beardsley, nephew of Havilah Beardsley, joined the firm as its first true manager. He had shown his executive abilities with the Muzzy Starch Company, and as city clerk and city treasurer. Thus, the third of the three most important and influential families in the history of Miles Laboratories (Miles, Compton, and Beardsley) had joined the company. At that time, Beardsley and his wife, Elizabeth (daughter of Silas Baldwin), lived in a lovely home on High Street, which later became the Four Arts Club.

In 1891 the Miles Medical Company built a three story building on the south side of Franklin Street, immediately west of the alley between Main and Second streets. The building housed printing and packaging departments, in addition to the medical production areas and offices. The printing department was responsible for developing and sending out Dr. Miles' medical journals.

This picture of the first building built for Miles Medical Company, located on the south side of Franklin Street, between Main and Second, was taken about 1892.

The Miles Medical Company office force in 1892, standing in front of their new building on Franklin Street. The man standing fifth from the right is Albert R. Beardsley, Chief Executive and Treasurer.

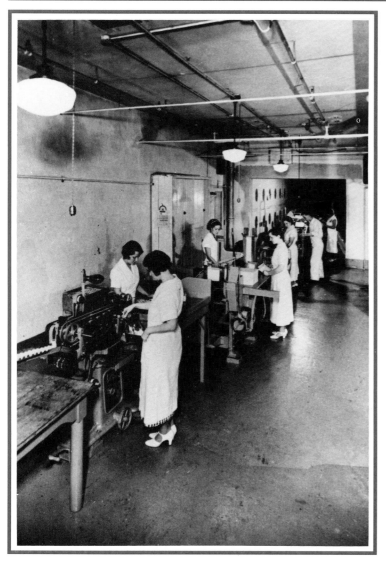

Workers packaging products inside Miles Medical Company on Franklin Street.

By 1903 annual sales of the Miles Medical Company had reached $700,000, and 160 men and women were in the employ of Dr. Miles. But he was not satisfied with just making and selling medicine. He also maintained his medical practice, in a large dispensary, at the corner of Main and Pratt (now Marion) streets.

In 1893 he moved the dispensary to Chicago, to the Masonic Temple Building, which was the tallest building in the world at that time. He took his three teenaged children with him to Chicago, and in 1895 married his attractive young assistant, Elizabeth State (who was also from Elkhart). While in Chicago, Miles retained his presidency of the medical company in Elkhart, and kept in touch with it, mostly by mail.

Shortly after 1900, Dr. Miles returned to Elkhart, establishing his dispensary in the Bucklen Opera House building. But after several spells of illness, he left the dispensary in the care of his son, Charles, and left for Florida with his wife. There he began a new career as a pioneer in the scientific cultivation of vegetables.

While he continued to be in touch with his medical company, and to be consulted by its officers, daily operations were carried on by others. General Manager A. R. Beardsley began to rely, more and more, on his nephew, Andrew Hubble Beardsley, who started with Miles as a bottle washer, and rose quickly to company secretary. After the deaths of A. R. Beardsley in 1924 and Dr. Miles in 1929, "Hub" Beardsley became chairman of the board, and president.

Miles Laboratories has experienced a great deal of growth over the years, but one of its most spectacular

The expanded Miles Laboratories on Franklin Street. At the right is the Monger Building, an office building that was built on the southeast corner of Second and Franklin, and was long a landmark in Elkhart. This building replaced the old Monger home, which Charles Monger had bought from John McNaughton. Both the Miles and Monger buildings were torn down to make way for the new St. Joseph Valley Bank (now NBD Midwest Commerce Banking Company).

THE HOME OF DR. MILES' REMEDIES
ELKHART IND.

examples of rapid growth resulted from the introduction of Alka-Seltzer in 1931, and the advertising campaign that made it a household word around the nation. Alka-Seltzer sales in 1933 reached $400,000. In 1934 sales were $2 million. In 1935 the figure was $5 million, and in 1936 sales reached $7.5 million. All this was in the midst of the Great Depression!

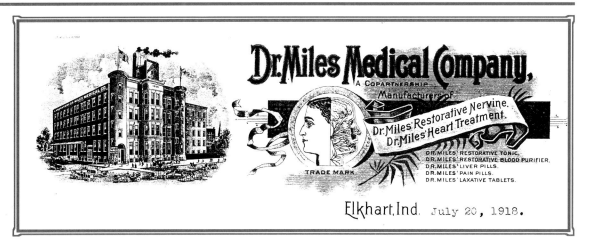

In 1935 an export division opened, and in 1938 the company moved from Franklin Street to new, much larger facilities in the northwest section of town, its present location on Myrtle Street. Dr. Walter Ames Compton, grandson of George Compton, joined the firm that year. Later, he was president and chief executive officer, and was responsible for turning the attention of the company to scientific development.

In 1978 Miles Laboratories was purchased by Bayer AG of Leverkusen, Germany, for $253 million. By 1984 there were 12,000 employees (2700 locally), and yearly sales were over $1 billion.

A 1906 advertisement for Dr. Miles' Nervine.

"Speedy Alka-Seltzer" was used in many advertisements over the years, and was known nation-wide, as well as in other countries.

THE FIRE DEPARTMENT

During the early days in Elkhart, there was no established fire department. When a fire was discovered, everyone who could do so joined in a bucket brigade, forming a line from the nearest river to the scene of the fire. A hand pump engine was purchased from Indianapolis in February of 1861, but it was returned a year later, due to the fact that it was too heavy to be used on the dirt streets of Elkhart. Late in 1867, a Silsby steam fire engine, with a hose cart and hose, was purchased, and a shed located on East Pigeon Street (Lexington) was bought to house the engine. Cisterns were dug at various locations to sup-ply water for the steam engine. In January of 1868, John Cassler was hired as the first paid fireman. His job was to run the steam engine, for which he was paid twenty dollars a month.

When Elkhart became a city, in 1875, Edward A. Campbell was appointed to be the first City Fire Chief. The fire station was located in the first City Hall building, on the northeast corner of High and Second streets. In 1886 a fire alarm system was installed in Elkhart, with ten alarm boxes in various parts of the city, in spite of the fact that the mayor tried to prevent it's installation. He thought the city would have a difficult time paying for it. In October, 1893, the fire department was reorganized and put on a paid (rather

Elkhart's first steam fire engine, shown here in the early 1880s, in front of the fire station on the northeast corner of High and Second streets. Beside it are two hose reels.

Inside the fire department (located in the City Hall building on High Street) in 1896, shortly before the fire station moved to East Franklin Street. The firemen (from left to right) are Charles Wilcox, William Eller (on wagon), John Ulrich, Alex Dotson, Algie Darling, Charles Sanford (on wagon), and Frank Little.

than volunteer) basis. In 1896 the fire department moved to the new City Hall building on East Franklin, near the Elkhart River.

As the city's size and population grew, so did its fire-fighting needs. In 1904 Fire Station No. 2 was built at the northeast corner of Main and Prairie streets, and in October of that year, Elkhart discontinued the use of volunteer fireman. In 1905 two more stations were built, Station No. 3 at the Northeast corner of Oakland and Mason, and Station No. 4 at the northeast corner of Beardsley and Plum. When the C. G. Conn company burned to the ground in 1910, city officials were prompted to purchase the first motorized pumper. Before the truck could be delivered,

the Star Match factory was also destoyed by fire. By 1916 all the fire-fighting vehicles used in Elkhart were motorized.

Other innovations were introduced over the years in order to keep Elkhart's fire department up to date. A new fire alarm system was put into operation in 1929. Miles Laboratories donated a panel truck to be used as the first fire department ambulance in 1942. Two-way radios were installed on all departmental units in 1943. By 1957 three-way radios were being used by all fire department vehicles, and Elkhart had 84 firemen. In 1972 Elkhart became the first fire department in Indiana (and the third in the nation) to have a paramedic system which met federal standards.

Mag and Fan, locally-famous horses of the Elkhart Fire Department, are shown here in front of "their" fire station, located at the northeast corner of Beardsley and Plum. The horses were purchased in 1892. They died tragically from injuries received, when they were hit by a streetcar in front of the station during a practice run, on January 22, 1908.

Elkhart firemen who lost their lives in the line of duty:

Earl Garl	1908
Frederick Shigley	1913
Ed Clark	1948
Henry Wisolek	1951
Terry Crouch	1972
Gerald Freed	1972
Carl Rheinheimer	1974
Rick Genth	1981

This building was used to store a hose cart for the fire department. It was located about where Volcano Pizza is now, in Easy Shopping Place. This picture was taken about 1904 from an upper story window of the C. G. Conn factory, looking northeast. The hydraulics (water raceways), used to power various factories, can be seen in the background.

Fire station number three, shown here about 1906, at the northeast corner of Oakland and Mason, was built in 1905 and torn down in 1926, to make room for Lincoln School. The man driving (holding a whip) is Earl Garl, first man to die in the line of duty for the Elkhart Fire Department. Beside him is Capt. August Stocker. The man standing at the far right is Art Carper. To his left is Frank Robinson.

Central fire station at 135 East Franklin, shortly before motorization of the Elkhart Fire Department began. B. F. Leader (later Mayor of Elkhart) was Chief at the time.

The fully motorized Elkhart Fire Department in 1916, at the corner of High and Second streets. The Chief's car is a Ford Runabout, followed by a Webb Pumper, a Seagrave City Service Ladder Truck, and Ford Truck Hose Wagons.

Looking west from the corner of Franklin and Main streets about 1910, during a practice drill, using the new motor fire engine (on the left) and the horse-drawn ladder truck (on the right). The building on the right is Ziesel's department store. On the left is the First State Bank building, later the Pharmanette, then Walgreen's, and still later, the "new" Kresge's Dime Store. The intersection street light can be seen top center.

No. 2   No. 3   No. 4   Electrician

...rtment 1916 By Mudge.

A motorcycle club in the 1920's, in front of the Green Block (on the south side of East Lexington).

The west side of the 100 block of North Main Street in 1911. The store on the left is the Winer junk shop. Next to it is Personette Bicycle and Motorcycle, followed by Spicer Teas and Coffee, and the Second Hand Furniture Store, and above it, Turner Hospital (from 1907 to 1911). Paul Thomas Shoes now occupies the two store fronts shown on the right, and Paul Thomas' "Time Was" museum is upstairs over his store.

The Martin Bus Line serving Elkhart, Wakarusa, and Nappanee, about 1910.

The Elkhart Baking
Company, located at 1315
Princeton, about the turn of
the century.

Curtis Upholstering and Picture Framing, located at
422 South Main Street in 1901.

ELKHART HOTELS

Hotels have played an important and sometimes-colorful role in the history of Elkhart. Little has been recorded about the earliest hotels, the first of which was built before 1834, near the east end of Washington Street, close to the mouth of the Elkhart River. It was called the Elkhart Exchange. At first there was very little difference between taverns and inns (hotels) in Elkhart.

The second hotel was located on the southeast corner of Main and Jackson. There, Col. Stephen Downing built a hostelry in 1834. It was torn down to make way for the DeFreese house, which burned down in 1852. A year later, J. R. Beardsley and his brother-in-law, B. L. Davenport, built a new hotel on this site and called it Clifton House. In 1860 it was destroyed by fire. In 1863 Silas Baldwin joined Beardsley and Davenport in erecting still another hotel on the same site. It, too, was named Clifton House, and in the 1880's was sold to H. E. Bucklen. He renovated it and renamed it the Hotel Bucklen.

Other early hotels were "Tammany Hall," built in 1836 on the southwest corner of Main and Jefferson, and the Elkhart House, built on the southeast corner of Second and Jackson in 1843.

In addition, there were many boardinghouses in Elkhart. One of the more interesting ones was a building called "The Railroad," built in 1856, on the northwest corner of Harrison and Main, reached from the main part of town by a path through the woods. It

Hotel Elkhart, located on the southeast corner of Main and Marion, was built in 1924.

Built in 1888 at the southeast corner of Main and Division, the Central Block Building first housed the Hotel Golden, with rooms costing one dollar per day, or four dollars per week.

was owned by Eli and Mary Hilton. This means that, though it wasn't known as such, there was once an Elkhart Hilton hotel! It was replaced in 1884 by the Bucklen Opera House.

Over the years, quite a few hotels were built in the vicinity of the railroad station, including the New Kaiserhof and the Travelers Depot hotels, which were located next to each other on Tyler Avenue, in what is now parking space for mail trucks and post office patrons. The Depot Hotel had 45 rooms, ten of which had private baths, and old-timers liked to sit on the porch and watch the dozens of trains come and go. A number of hotels have occupied the Central Block building at the southeast corner of Main and Harrison, since it was built in 1888.

The Hotel Elkhart, perhaps the best known and most respected hotel in downtown Elkhart in recent times, was built in 1924, and was the scene of many fashionable balls and parties. In 1974 Hotel Elkhart was purchased by the Mennonite Board of Missions, and renamed the Greencroft Center. It is now a local retirement apartment complex, the name having been changed to Greencroft Tower Apartments in 1986.

The New Kaiserhof Hotel, on the north side of Tyler Avenue, west of Main Street, was known for its excellent German food and closeness to town.

The Travelers Depot Hotel was located on Tyler Avenue, one building west of the New Kaiserhof Hotel.

The lobby and check-in desk of the Hotel Bucklen, located on the southeast corner of Main and Jackson, around 1900.

On the north side of East Jackson, just a block past Main Street, was the B.C. Godfrey Coal Company, in 1910. The coal cars would go up into the structure at the right and then let the coal fall out through openings in the bottom of the rail cars into wagons waiting below.

This picture taken in front of the Electric Company on Lexington Avenue, shows goose-egg sized hail stones that fell on July 11, 1911.

Inside the Irvin Potts saloon on Tyler Avenue, across from the New York Central depot, about the turn of the century.

The driver of the Lusher Brothers' Number 3 wagon pauses for a picture beside the Soldiers and Sailors monument, at the corner of Tyler and Main, about 1899.

MONUMENTS

In the 1880's, a feeling arose in Elkhartans that some sort of memorial should be erected in honor of the soldiers and sailors who died in the Civil War. Silas Baldwin offered to build a monument in honor of all Civil War veterans, and in memory of his son, Lt. Frank Baldwin, who was killed at age 18 in the Battle of Stone River, on December 31, 1862.

Plans were made for the monument to be unveiled on the day of its dedication, August 23, 1889, at the intersection of Main Street and Tyler Avenue. Silas Baldwin, the man who had made it all possible, died before the finished monument was unveiled. The dedication came about as scheduled, with Indiana Governor Alvin P. Hovey delivering the address for the occasion.

As automobiles began to replace horse-drawn vehicles and to greatly increase in numbers, the monument was considered to be a traffic hazard in that location. So when the new sewer was put down and Main Street was resurfaced in the spring of 1928, the monument was moved to Rice Cemetery. In May of 1910, a similar but smaller monument was unveiled at Grace Lawn Cemetery.

Looking north from the monument at Main and Tyler streets. All the buildings to the left of the Bucklen Opera House on the west side of the 600 block of South Main Street were torn down in 1964 to make way for the new post office. The boys crossing the street in front of the monument are wearing knickers. This picture was taken about 1905.

Looking south on Main Street from the monument about 1924 shows the beginning of the traffic problem. The small, white, elevated structure, to the right of the building at the far left, is the post from which a railroad employee used to raise and lower the crossing gates when trains approached the Main Street and Middlebury crossings. The spires of St. Vincent's Catholic Church and St. James A.M.E. Church can be seen above the trees on the horizon.

The Puterbaugh Block, on the west side of the 300 block of South Main Street, is the name of the tall building shown here, about 1883. Kavanagh and Pollard's grocery store is to the right of it.

The building on the right is the old Jenner Drug Store. It was originally called the Cornish Building, and is still standing on the southwest corner of Main and Lexington. Henry T. Jenner, owned the store from 1910 to 1923, and his son, Alfred D. Jenner, from 1923 to 1967. Booths in the rear of the store, where friends could sip cherry phosphates or ice cream sodas, were a favorite spot for refreshment "in the old days."

The Century Club building was erected in 1898 on the west side of Main Street, just north of Jackson, by H. E. Bucklen. It cost $20,000 (including furnishings) and was a center for social events for many years, later known as the Atherton Club.

The Monger Building, long a familiar office building in downtown Elkhart, was built on the southeast corner of Franklin and Second in 1904. A fifth story was added in 1907 to provide space for the Superior Court, until it could be relocated in the Municipal Building in 1916. In this picture, taken about 1910, the old Miles Medical Company building can be seen at the far left. Both buildings were torn down in 1971 to make way for the new St. Joseph Valley Bank.

The old Elks' Temple, in 1910, on the east side of the 300 block of South Main Street. The sign in the window of Turnocks' (later the site of Goldberg's Men's Store) says, "$1.00 a week is as good as cash." In 1978 all the buildings in this picture were demolished making room for the Midway Motor Lodge.

This is a northward view of Main Street about 1924, from the top of the Hotel Elkhart. Main Street at that time had diagonal parking on both sides of the street, two-way traffic, and streetcars.

The Kane Lodge of Free and Accepted Masons was formed in Elkhart in 1855. The first Masonic Temple building appeared in 1871 at 115 South Main Street. Due to increased membership, the Masons met on the third floor of the Bucklen Opera House building from 1893 to 1900, moving in early 1900 to the third floor of what became the Ziesel's building. Continued membership growth necessitated a building to house all Masonic Bodies and activities. So, in 1910, Brother E. Hill Turnock, a member of Kane Lodge, was chosen as the architect for the Masonic Temple (pictured here), which still stands on the east side of Second Street between Jackson and Lexington. The building was first used in early 1911.

This is what Waterfall Drive looked like about 1900, shortly after the police and fire station (City Hall) was built. It can be seen at the top right in this picture. At the top left is the old iron Elkhart Avenue bridge. At that time, it was called the Franklin Street bridge because Franklin went all the way out to Jackson Boulevard.

Looking north on North Sixth Street from Lexington Avenue during the flood in the spring of 1900.

Snow is falling in downtown Elkhart in December of 1950, in the 400 block of South Main Street, looking north. "The Tanks are Coming" is the movie playing at the Elco theater.

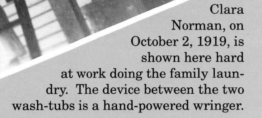

Clara Norman, on October 2, 1919, is shown here hard at work doing the family laundry. The device between the two wash-tubs is a hand-powered wringer.

Dr. and Mrs. Frederick C. Eckleman are shown standing in front of their house at 219 South Second Street, about 1900. The house was located next to the Municipal Building, and was torn down in 1951.

This picture, taken around 1910, shows an auto race about to begin on Main Street. The white building, on the northeast corner of Main and Jefferson streets, is John Landon's automobile garage, which later became the Armory.

Emma Zilky Grant is seen here, on December 25,1904, in her fancy hat.

John Weiler and friends pose for a "gag" photo in the early 1920's. This type of picture was often used as a business or calling card, or a post card, and printed on very stiff paper.

Earl Garl, who was the first Elkhart fireman to be killed in the line of duty.

George Rowe, getting ready to ride his bicycle in 1896, receives a little support from an unidentified friend.

A picture of the entire Elkhart Public Schools teaching staff, taken in 1899, outside Elkhart High School (later Samuel Strong School). Everyone wore numbers for identification. Superintendent D. W. Thomas is Number 1; High School Principal S. B. McCracken is Number 9. To the right of him is Mary Beck, Number 5. At the far left, in the front row, is Clara Van Nuys, Number 28. At the left, in the second row from the top, is Mary Daly, Number 29.

Teddy Roosevelt making a whistle-stop at the Main Street railroad crossing in Elkhart in 1912.

A classroom of students in old Central school. This picture was taken on Friday, January 25, 1907. The teacher, Miss Bliss, is standing by the blackboard on the right.

Berman's Sporting Goods store at 129 South Main Street about 1930.

Inside Berman's Sporting Goods store about 1930.

THE ARMORY

The building at the northeast corner of Main and Jefferson streets is most commonly known as The Armory. Originally a blacksmith shop stood on this spot. In 1905 the shop was converted into the first public automobile garage in Elkhart, by John S. Landon, who came here that year from Kokomo. A year later, the original building was torn down. Herbert E. Bucklen replaced it with what became the south half of the present building. Then, in 1911, Bucklen doubled the size of the building, to provide an armory for the local company of the national guard. E. Hill Turnock was in charge of planning the expansion, and the remodeling of the front of the building. The property was bought from the Bucklen estate by John W. Fieldhouse in 1922. Over the years, the building has housed a number of businesses. For a long time, the A & P grocery store occupied the main floor, while the upstairs was used as a rollerskating rink.

The former blacksmith shop was converted to Elkhart's first full-time automobile service garage in 1905. In the car on the left, are R. Ray Beardsley (son of J. R. Beardsley), his wife, Gertrude, and their son, Rufus. John Landon is in the car on the right, and his assistant, Harry Beck, is in the car in the middle which belonged to C.G. Conn. Donald Graham is standing near the front of the Beardsley car.

This building, erected in 1906, for John Landon's expanding business, was the south half of what became the Armory, at the northeast corner of Main and Jefferson.

The Elkhart Armory, looking nearly the same as it does today.

Mrs. Mary Landon, at age 94, standing by an 1897 Haynes-Apperson horseless carriage. In 1897, while she was a stenographer for the Haynes-Apperson Motor Wagon Company in Kokomo, she became the first woman in America to drive a gasoline-powered automobile. Eight years later Mrs. Landon and her husband, John, moved to Elkhart. They left Elkhart in 1912, but after John's death, she and their two sons, Keith and Jack, returned to Elkhart in 1927.

ELKHART BUSINESSES

Emil G. Krienke's merchant tailor store, located at 216 South Main Street, is shown here in the summer of 1886. The sidewalk in those days was literally a boardwalk.

The store on the right is The Fair, later called Mc The Fair. On the left is Stephens' furniture and undertaking business.

In 1910, when this picture was taken, the American Veneer and Roofing Company was located at 564 East Jackson Boulevard. The plant manufactured veneer roofing, and used 75 tons of paper and 75 tons of asphalt annually. The waterway seen here is a tail race, through which water flowed after it had been used to provide hydraulic power for the manufacturing process.

Some workers posing outside the Elkhart Bridge and Iron Company, on the southwest corner of Michigan and Mishawaka streets, about 1915. The company was founded around 1895 by Frank Brumbaugh, and was originally called Elkhart Bridge Company. It was moved to its present location in 1904, but due to decreased demand for its products, went out of business in the summer of 1983.

Located on the southwest corner of Ren and Sterling streets, the H. W. Gossard Corset Company began manufacturing corsets in 1907. This picture was taken about 1910.

This picture of Shreiner and Heffner Contractors, located at 522 South Main Street, was taken about 1890. Two of their delivery wagons are standing in front of the establishment. The Crescent Cafe is next door, on the right.

Two delivery trucks are shown here, in 1916, at 744 South Main, in front of the Mishler-Henderson 20th Century Garage, which was also a Republic Motor Truck agency. An advertisement for Pillsbury flour and White House coffee can be seen on the sideboards of the Twin City Grocer Company truck.

The Chicago Telephone Supply Company (now called CTS) began in Chicago in 1896. It moved to Elkhart in 1902, after the City of Elkhart offered the company a new factory building, with 34,000 square feet of space, a steam-heating plant, a spur railroad track, five acres of land, and all expenses paid for the move from Chicago. In return, the company agreed to hire enough workers to pay out $300,000 in wages, which it did (within the first three years in Elkhart). This aerial view of CTS, taken in 1958, shows how much growth the company has experienced since its move to Elkhart.

This picture of the Bucklen Livery, at 117 East Lexington Avenue, was taken about 1905. The business was established in 1900, and provided accomodations for 100 horses. Later, the Red Crown Bowling Alley occupied this building, until it was gutted by a fire in 1963. In the spring of 1979, the building was torn down to provide a parking lot for First National Bank employees.

This picture, taken about 1900, shows the Felthouse Brothers grocery store. It was located at 1002 Middlebury Street, next to Grace Lawn Cemetery.

This building, still standing at 125 East Lexington Avenue, was built in 1895 for the National Paper and Supply Company. In 1908 the Twin City Grocer Company moved into this building, and remained there for about seventeen years.

In 1880 the Elkhart Paper Box factory, owned by Alfred C. Cowherd and Frank A. Weatherwax, was located on East High Street. Seven years later, the firm was bought by William Barger and his son, W. H. Barger, and eventually moved to East Franklin Street. Today, Barger Packaging Corporation is located on West Lusher Avenue, and is still producing paperboard (and plastic) packaging products. This picture was taken around 1900, after the company moved to Franklin Street.

POST OFFICE

The first post office, in what is now Elkhart, was established June 6, 1829, in the little settlement of Pulaski, near the mouth of Christiana Creek. George Crawford was the first postmaster. At first the job was not too arduous. There were only a few settlers, and the mail came once a month, then every two weeks, later every week. The mail carrier was known as "old man Hall" and arrived on horseback from Fort Wayne. There was no home delivery. U. S. postage stamps did not exist prior to 1847. In order to get a letter (since prepayment of postage was not required), the one receiving the letter often had to pay twenty-five cents.

The post office was moved south of the St. Joseph River about 1835, and its name was changed to Elkhart

This is the first building erected to be a post office in Elkhart. It was built in 1868 and is still standing on the north side of the 100 block of West Jackson. The *Elkhart Daily Review* was published on the second floor. For many years, this building has been Martin's Pet and Garden Center.

When the post office was moved to this building on the southeast corner of Main and Franklin, the first victory for the south-siders was won. The post office was located here from 1886 until 1905, and it was from this post office that free mail delivery began.

George Rowe, shown here with his son, Chester, was a letter carrier for 38 years, from 1895 until 1933. After being a substitute mailman for three years, he was made a regular carrier on a "mounted" route, which meant that he had to supply his own horse and wagon.

in 1839, on petition by Havilah Beardsley. This post office was first located in a little wooden building, on the west side of Main Street, midway between Jackson and Jefferson. For the next 33 years, the location of the post office would vary according to where the local merchant, who had been appointed postmaster, happened to have his place of business. In 1868 the first building intended to be a post office in Elkhart was erected, on the north side of Jackson Boulevard. It was located west of the alley between Main and Second streets. The construction cost $14,000. This appeared to settle a long-standing question between the north-siders and the south-siders, as to which end of town would have the honor and the convenience of the post office.

However, in 1886, the post office was moved to the southeast corner of Main and Franklin, and it now appeared that the south-siders had won. It was at this time that free mail delivery was started in the city, with four carriers and a substitute. In 1905, in response to a feeling that a bigger, government-owned building was needed, the post office was moved north once again, to the northwest corner of Main and Jackson. This building cost $85,000. The post office remained in it for 60 years.

In 1965 Elkhart's population had increased to where the sheer volume of mail each day, and technological advances in mail processing, required that a new building be built. And so, the post office was moved back south, to the block bounded by Main, Tyler, Second, and Harrison streets.

This is the northwest corner of Main and Jackson in 1898. The long building on the left, in the foreground, was occupied by Homer Brown's bicycle shop. Fulton's Fish Market is just west of it, on Jackson. The building on the far left, with enclosed stairs going up the outside, is the first building built to be a post office in Elkhart. To the right of Homer Brown's is the Beebe home (with a white door). It was torn down shortly after this picture was taken, in order to construct the Century Club building. Mrs. Rosalie Beebe taught the first Sunday School in her home, which was built in 1832 by her husband, Judge Samuel P. Beebe. It was the second house built in the village of Elkhart, south of the St. Joseph River, and was located on this same lot. Before he became a judge, Samuel Beebe opened the first mercantile business in the platted village of Elkhart, on the southeast corner of Main and Jackson. His business was replaced by Col. Stephen Downing's hotel, in turn replaced by the Clifton House. On the left side of the billboard, in the foreground, is a sign that says, "War News," referring to the Spanish-American War.

This picture of the northwest corner of Main and Jackson was taken in 1903, shortly before the building on the left, housing Homer Brown's bicycle shop, was torn down to make way for the new post office. The building on the right is the Century Club, built in 1898. It was the scene of many festive social events, and had a large ballroom on the third floor. In later years, it was a furniture store, and has since been demolished. Hitching posts can be seen along Main Street in front of the buildings.

In 1905 the newly-completed post office was an imposing structure, on the northwest corner of Main and Jackson. The old post office can be seen on the left, and the Century Club on the right. Having been remodeled by Valley American Bank, the 1905 post office building remains a landmark today.

LIBRARY

The Elkhart Public Library had its roots in the Ladies' Library Association, which, in 1874, formed a subscription library with a public reading room. In 1901 Andrew Carnegie agreed to donate $35,000 for a public library in Elkhart, and by 1903 Elkhart Carnegie Library opened on the northeast corner of Second and High. Miss Katherine Sage was appointed to be the first librarian. Elkhart's first bookmobile was donated by Mrs. A. H. Beardsley in 1921. However, it was sold for $75 in 1930, due to the depression, and because of a need to cover operating costs. Bookmobile service was resumed in 1948. Fifteen years later, when Miss Ruth Kellog was librarian, the Elkhart Public Library moved to its present building on the southeast corner of Second and High, which was made possible by the Martin Foundation.

The Elkhart Carnegie Library was built on the northeast corner of Second and High, in 1903. It was torn down in 1970, and replaced by a parking lot for First National Bank.

Elkhart's first bookmobile, shown here in front of the Carnegie Library, was donated by Mrs. A. H. Beardsley in 1921. The boy on the left is wearing an apron that says, "The Saturday Evening Post" and "The Country Gentleman," two prominent magazines of the time.

A view of the children's department of the Carnegie Library, which was located in the south end of the main floor, in 1903. The edge of the check-out desk can be seen at the far left. Later, the children's department was moved downstairs.

The check-out desk on the main floor of the Carnegie Library in 1903. The arch, at the far right, led to the stairway to the upper stacks. The upper level had a thick, stained glass floor.

The present Elkhart Public Library, located on the southeast corner of Second and High streets, was built in 1963, as a result of the Martin Foundation donating the necessary funds.

STREETCARS

The Citizens' Street Railway Company was organized in 1886 to provide a horse car line for the city of Elkhart. The first streetcars were drawn by horses or mules. At that time, Elkhart was one of thirteen Indiana cities with mule-powered streetcars.

Three years later, in 1889, Elkhart became the second city in the world to have an electric streetcar system. Tracks were laid in the following locations: along Main Street from Beardsley Avenue, Middlebury Street to Grace Lawn Cemetery, Jackson Boulevard to the Big Four Railroad Station, Marion Street and Franklin Street to the bridge, and West Beardsley Avenue to Michigan Street. By 1889 there were seven miles of track laid in Elkhart: crossing Bridge Street bridge past Highland (McNaughton) Park, along Vine Street to Bower Street, and east to the Sherman Street bridge.

The original streetcar barns were located in the first block east of Main Street, on the north side of

Looking north, from the corner of Main and Marion streets in 1887, a horse-drawn streetcar can be seen. The building on the left has a sign on it that says,"Occidental Dining Hall." It was later a bank, and still later, the site of the old St. Joseph Valley Bank, now the Midwest Museum of Art. At the right is a fair grounds and picnic area, where Hotel Elkhart (now Greencroft Center) was later built. In this picture, Main Street is still unpaved.

Elkhart's first electric streetcars, shown here at the original car barn on East Jackson, in 1889.

Jackson Boulevard. Later, they were moved to the northwest corner of South Main and Lusher, to the building now occupied by Dexter Axle Company.

On December 21, 1898, the first interurban passenger cars, very similar in appearance to streetcars, traveled from Elkhart to Goshen. The first interurban service between Elkhart and South Bend began in January, 1900. Herbert E. Bucklen bought and expanded an interurban railway company, that eventually stretched out East Jackson beyond Bristol, Middlebury, LaGrange, and Angola, to a terminal in Columbus, Ohio. This service ended when Bucklen died in 1917.

Streetcars were a convenience for many, and are now a nostalgic memory for those who recall riding in them. On Saturday, June 2, 1934, the Elkhart streetcars made their final runs. That last day was free to anyone who wanted to ride, and two days later, city bus service began. In August of 1939, the streetcar tracks down Main Street were taken out by WPA workmen.

The second streetcar barn, located at the corner of Main and Lusher, is now occupied by the Dexter Axle Company.

A normally busy day for streetcars, about 1905, as seen from the corner of Main and Marion, looking northwest,.

A lone streetcar approaching the corner of Main and Hickory streets from the north, about 1905.

A view of Main Street from the
corner of Harrison, looking
north about 1905.

Looking west on Marion from the intersection at Main Street. The large building on the right is The Citizens Trust Company, a bank owned by Dr. Franklin Miles. Midwest Museum of Art now occupies that site. This picture was taken about 1914.

The interurban station on the south side of West Marion Street, west of the alley between Second and Third streets, about 1905. Later, it became an American Legion home. The interurban car on the right is ready to head towards Goshen.

The Surface Car Terminal, at the corner of Main and Marion (looking south), about 1905.

Looking south from the Bucklen Opera House (at the corner of Main and Harrison), about 1905. The buildings on the right have been torn down to make room for the new post office. The building, marked "Hotel Golden" (on the left), was built in 1888, and is still standing.

BRIDGES

This is a picture of the first iron bridge to Island Park, from the east end of Sycamore Street. It was originally half of the Main Street bridge, from 1871 until 1891.

This is a view of the old Pigeon Street (Lexington Avenue) bridge, looking west in 1912. It is the bridge that elephants (in circus parades) didn't like to cross, due to its tendency to sway or "bounce" when marching bands, crowds, or heavy loads crossed over it. The circus grounds were located on the south side of Lexington Avenue, west of the bridge, in what was called Johnson Commons. The elephants would wade or swim across the St. Joseph River. If they refused to do either, they would have to be marched back up Pigeon Street to Main, cross the Main Street bridge, and come clear around Front Street (Riverside Drive) to Johnson Commons.

A picture of the first wooden bridge built to Island Park from the mainland, about 1887.

Below is a picture of the Six Span Bridge, east of Elkhart, when it really had six wooden spans. Later this bridge was replaced by a four span iron bridge (with longer spans), but retained its old name. It was replaced by a modern, concrete bridge, in 1968.

An aerial view of the present Johnson Street bridge, showing the dam over the St. Joseph River, just to the left (east) of the bridge, and the railroad bridge crossing, near the mouth of Christiana Creek, to the right. The diagonal road, heading to the southwest at the top right of the picture, is Elkhart Avenue, and the buildings above it are part of Easy Shopping Place. East Beardsley Avenue runs left to right across the bottom of the picture. Originally, Beardsley Avenue was interrupted (from Johnson Street west to Cassopolis) by the Lane-Erwin paper mill.

ZIESEL'S

Silas Baldwin came to Elkhart in 1843 to manage the P. P. Mailliard store. He bought the store a year later and operated it until 1856, at which time he entered into the banking business with Philo Morehous. By the time the Bank of Elkhart became First National Bank, in 1864, Baldwin was first cashier. He was postmaster from 1844 until 1848, and was instrumental in bringing the railroad to Elkhart, which resulted in his being appointed the first local station agent for the railroad company. Silas and his wife, Jane, had two children, Frank, an Army Lieutenant who was killed in the battle of Stone River in 1862, and Elizabeth, who later married A. R. Beardsley.

The home of Silas and Jane Baldwin, on the northwest corner of Main and Franklin, was torn down in 1901 and replaced by a large retail business building. At the time it was torn down, it was the next to the last residential property left on the west side of Main Street, between Jackson and the railroad tracks. In this picture, the steeple of Trinity Methodist Church can be seen in the distance, immediately to the left of the house, while the white picket fence is a reminder of the first residential picket fences on Main Street. The fences were put up to keep pigs out of private yards and gardens. Pigs, in the early days of the village, were allowed to roam freely, even in the "downtown" area.

The Baldwin Block, on the northwest corner of Main and Franklin, was also known as the Beardsley Block, because Elizabeth Baldwin Beardsley owned it. Between 1901 and 1904, the building was occupied by two retail businesses. Vinnedges Dry Goods House was in the south end of the building, while Mc The Fair was in the north end. The Elks club met on the second floor. While there were a few automobiles in Elkhart at this time, hitching posts can still be seen lining both Main and Franklin streets.

In 1904 Mc The Fair was bought by the Ziesel brothers, Conrad and Edward. Conrad was three years old when his family came to Elkhart in 1859. At age 15, he became a clerk in A. R. Beardsley's dry goods store. Later, he worked for J. F. Hunt and for H. B. Sykes, also as a clerk. Four years after the Ziesel brothers opened a store of their own, they bought out the Boyle and Brown store, directly to the south, where Vinnedges Dry Goods House had been. In 1912 an elevator was installed when the store expanded to the third floor.

The Ziesel Brothers department store established the first motorized truck delivery service in Elkhart, in 1911. In this picture Clarence Ziesel is on the right. The other man is Charley Clipp.

E. Hill Turnock

E. Hill Turnock,
Elkhart architect.

The name of one architect always comes to mind-when architecture is thought about in Elkhart. E. Hill Turnock (The E. stands for Enock.) has left an indelible mark on the architectural scene here. Even though at least ten of the Elkhart landmarks which he designed have been demolished, there remain some seventy homes and other buildings in Elkhart, for which he was the architect.

Born in London, England, in 1857, Turnock came to Elkhart with his parents in 1872. As a young man in Elkhart, he worked as a patternmaker for the Lake Shore railroad, eventually becoming head patternmaker. At the age of 30, he got a job in Chicago with an architectural firm, where he helped design the first steel skyscraper in that city. Later, he worked for architect Frank Lloyd Wright. In 1907, after returning to Elkhart, he began a highly prolific period in his career, until his death in 1926.

The structures he designed, which have since been torn down, include the old Elkhart High School, the former Christian Science Church, the Home Telephone

The old Home Telephone Company, designed by Turnock and located immediately east of the public restrooms on Franklin. This building was used for office space by Ziesel's, after the new telephone company was built on the corner of Second and Lexington, and was torn down in 1986.

This is a picture of the public restrooms building on the north side of the 100 block of West Franklin, designed by Turnock.

building, the public restrooms building on Franklin Street, the Firestone building (originally the Smith Ford garage) on the southeast corner of Second and Jackson, the former Elkhart Truth building on Second Street, the domed Presbyterian Church, Willowdale School, and the A. H. Beardsley home, next door to Ruthmere, on the west.

Still standing today are the Jefferson, Fleming Arms, and Warnell apartment houses, the last C. G. Conn factory, the Municipal Building, the Masonic Temple, the Communicana Building, the old YWCA,, the Armory, Borneman Hardware (now Sunthimer's), and the Water Works office. Turnock also designed the original portion of Elkhart General Hospital, and St. Paul's Methodist Church, as well as numerous other buildings. Among the many beautiful homes in Elkhart which he designed were, Ruthmere, the rectories of St. Paul's Methodist and St. John's Episcopal churches, the Heinheis (Foster) mansion, the Knickerbocker (Winchester) mansion, and at least 50 others. He also laid out Grace Lawn Cemetery.

Turnock did not limit himself to buildings and homes. He designed the monument to Havilah Beardsley, which is still standing where Riverside Drive and Beardsley Avenue meet.

E. Hill Turnock was the architect for the C. G. Conn factory on East Beardsley, built in 1910.

The City Water Works office was another of E. Hill Turnock's accomplishments.

THE "Y" STORY

The first YWCA, in 1911, was located at 319 West Marion.

In 1918 E. Hill Turnock was the architect for a new three story YWCA, at 120 West Lexington.

The Young Men's Christian Association (YMCA) began as a reading club in 1882, meeting in a room on Lexington Avenue, west of Main Street. Meetings were also held in second story and basement rooms in the 200 block of South Main Street. In 1884, the YMCA joined with the Lake Shore and Michigan Southern Railroad, and a building was erected on the south side of Tyler Avenue, directly east of the depot. It was open to railroad employees and the general public. The new building had a reading room, a gymnasium, baths, and classrooms. Due to lack of public support, the decision was made to build another building, limited to railroad employees.

The second railroad YMCA, located on the north side of Tyler, immediately west of Second Street, was built in 1904. It cost $25,000, of which $10,000 was contributed by the railroad, with the rest of the money being raised by railroad employees and local businessmen.

The Elkhart Community YMCA was organized in 1925, and a large building was built two years later, on the southeast corner of Third and Franklin streets. The structure included a gymnasium, a track for running, a large swimming pool, and ping-pong and pool tables. The third floor was reserved exclusively for railroad employees, until yet another Railroad YMCA was established, at the Robert E. Young Railroad Yards, from 1957 until 1983.

The Young Women's Christian Association (YWCA) began as a Bible reading group in 1908. At first, the meetings were held in the Monger Building, on the

The YMCA, located at the southeast corner of Third and Franklin, was a landmark in Elkhart from 1927 until 1974.

southeast corner of Second and Franklin. After affiliation with the state and national YWCA in 1908, the Elkhart YWCA made a move, in 1911, to its own building, located at 319 West Marion. In 1918 Mrs. Lizzie Compton donated a site at 120 West Lexington Avenue, on which a three story building, including a gymnasium and a cafeteria, was constructed. The cafeteria became a popular place to eat for many Elkhartans.

In 1973 the YMCA and the YWCA moved into a new, jointly-operated building at 200 East Jackson Boulevard. The old YMCA was torn down in 1974, and the old YWCA became a residential facility for Oaklawn Psychiatric Center.

The gymnasium (with overhead track), at the old YMCA on Franklin and Third, was the scene of many basketball games, as well as other athletic activities.

Many Elkhart boys learned to swim in the old YMCA pool. Because the YMCA was across Franklin Street from the High School Annex, it was also used by the Elkhart High School physical education department.

A high school affiliate of the YWCA, the Y-Teens, provided opportunities for community service for teenage girls in Elkhart. These included working for the Salvation Army, participating in World Fellowship Week, and sponsoring an Easter party. This picture, taken in 1958 at the old YWCA, shows the Y-Teens making plans for the annual Sweetheart Swing Dance. The third girl from the left (in the front) is Eleonora Gamma, an exchange student at Elkhart High School, from Brazil.

AUTOMOBILES

For nearly thirty years, Elkhart was actively involved in the manufacturing of automobiles. Sterling, Royal, Mercer, Sun, Menges, Shoemaker, St. Joe, Federal, Bush, Huffman, and Komet are all names of cars made in Elkhart at one time or another. Nearly 30 makes of cars were produced by at least 15 manufac-turers. The first car produced in Elkhart was a "horseless buggy" made by the Elkhart Carriage and Harness Manufacturing Company in 1906, as a "side line." This company, founded by F. B. Pratt in 1873, was known throughout the country for its horse-drawn vehicles, which were produced in the building still standing on the northwest corner of Beardsley Avenue and Michigan Street.

A 1916 advertisement for the new Elcar.

A group of workers inside the machine shop of the Crow-Elkhart Motor Car Company, about 1914.

The Crow Motor Car factory, on the southeast corner of North Main and Simonton streets, is now the Excel Company building.

By 1909 the Pratt-Elkhart automobile had become an established and profitable product. In 1916 the name of the company was changed to the Elkhart Carriage and Motor Car Company, and the name of the automobile to Elcar, probably the most well-known car ever made here. Two years later, due to a government emergency war order to produce ambulances, all carriage production came to a halt. The name of the company was changed to the Elcar Motor Company in 1922, and it continued in business until 1932.

Perhaps the next best known car made in Elkhart was the Crow-Elkhart, which was produced from 1909 until 1924. But a combination of competition, by larger automobile manufacturers, and the Great Depression, finally ended the production of automobiles in Elkhart, in 1935.

The three-passenger Roadster model of the 1921 Elcar.

Pictured below is the four-passenger Sportster, another model of the 1921 Elcar.

A horseless carriage approaching West Beardsley, about 1905. Leland Street is to the left, and Christiana Street straight ahead. The house on the left is 801 Christiana. The house on the right is 216 West Beardsley. Both are still standing.

Charles H. Winchester stands beside his new Cole automobile in 1914, outside the Second Street entrance to the new High School. This seven-passenger touring car featured electric lights, clincher wheels, and a klaxton horn. The car was made in Indianapolis and cost $5000. William H. Knickerbocker is sitting in the driver's seat. His mother-in-law, Mrs. C. H. (Elizabeth) Winchester is seated next to him. Nellie Knickerbocker, his wife, is in the back seat. The other man is unidentified.

The Frederick A. Blessing family in their car. This picture was taken in front of their house at 629 West Marion Street, about 1910. Frederick and his wife, Beulah, are in the front seat. In the back (from left to right) are Stanton, unknown, Ted, and an aunt.

This picture, taken on Middlebury Street about 1912, shows Vern Kemp and Eva Stamp Cathcart in the front seat of the car. In the back seat, from left to right are: Frances Kemp Anderson, Grandma Kemp, and Thelma Cathcart Hosler. The dog's name is Toots.

Joseph Masson and Homer F. Brown standing at the doorway of Homer Brown Bicycle Shop and Auto Supply, at 108 North Main Street, about 1914. Bricks have been placed on both sides of the rear wheel of the car in front of the store, apparently to keep the car from rolling either direction.

ELKHART HIGH SCHOOL

The Elkhart High School basketball team getting a sendoff to the Ft. Wayne Semi-State Tournament in 1960.

Nehemiah Broderick, the first school teacher in Elkhart, taught his students in a log cabin, which was built in 1836 on East Washington Street, near the south bank of the Elkhart River. A school was built in 1838 on the east side of Second Street, between Jackson and Washington, but it burned down in 1844. "Tammany Hall," built in 1844 on the southwest corner of Main and Jefferson, was used as a school for a period of time. In 1855, when a woman teacher, Mrs. A. E. Babb, was offered a teaching position at $30.00 per month, some local people felt it "an extravagance scarcely to be tolerated." In 1851 a school was built at the southwest corner of Second and High streets. It was a four story

frame building and burned down in 1867. At this point, the decision was made to build a four story brick building, large enough for all the grades and all the students in Elkhart. Completed in time for school to start in September, 1868, the building (referred to now as "Old Central") cost $45,000. Some local citizens protested that this new school was too extravagant, and furthermore, that there would never be enough students to fill it. However, only five years later, a new elementary school needed to be built, and was called Fourth Ward School (later Lincoln).

This same year (1873), the first Elkhart High School commencement exercises were held. Five students (all

Central School, on the southwest corner of Second and High, sometime between 1868 and 1880. The first high school classes were held here on the fourth floor. The old Trinity Methodist Church can be seen at far left. It was torn down in 1889.

Central School and the Annex, sometime between 1890 and 1907. The Trinity Methodist Church, which was built in 1889, can be seen on the left.

138

girls) graduated. Two of the graduates were the Simonton sisters. The following year, the graduating class consisted of only one student — a boy. After that, there were never fewer than three graduates per year. In those days, each graduate had to perform in some way at the commencement ceremonies to show how well educated he or she was. This normally consisted of an oration, or reading of an essay which the graduate had written.

By 1884 the population of Elkhart had reached about 7000, and there were 14 senior class graduates that year. A new eight room building, called the Annex, was built behind Old Central, on High Street. The high school and recitation rooms were located on the first floor, and the upper grammar grades on the second floor. The library, museum, and superintendent's office were in the area connecting the new and old buildings. The entire cost of the new building, including furniture, and the "steam-heating apparatus" used for both buildings, was $25,000. Five additional elementary schools had been built by 1884: Fifth Ward (replaced in 1921 by Roosevelt) and East Elkhart (replaced in 1925 by Rice) were built in 1875, Weston in 1878, Beardsley one year later, and Middlebury in 1883.

In 1884 Samuel S. Strong built a large new house (later the Conn mansion) on Strong Avenue, and gave

The first Elkhart High School, built in 1892, became Samuel Strong Elementary School in 1912. It is still standing at the intersection of Lexington and Vistula.

The front entrance to Elkhart High School, on High Street, in 1955. Not only students, but everyone who went to concerts, travelogues, and other events at the High School auditorium, or the old gymnasium, entered through these doors.

Elkhart High School in the 1950's.

the city the triangular property between Pigeon (Lexington) and Vistula, where his old house was located. On this property, in 1892, the first Elkhart High School was built. It was made of Indiana limestone and cost $35,000. The school contained four recitation rooms, a chemical laboratory, biological and physical science rooms, an assembly room that seated 200, a library with more than 5000 volumes, and the superintendent's office. The faculty consisted of Mr. Sylvester B. McCracken, principal and science teacher, Miss Clara Van Nuys, English teacher, Miss Ella Wilkinson, Latin teacher, and Mr. Morrison, mathematics teacher.

By 1890 the population of Elkhart had grown to 11,360, and South Side Elementary School had just been built. Ten years later, the size of the city had reached 15,184. It grew to 19,282 by 1910. Not surprisingly, the need for more classrooms continued to grow rapidly as well. In 1908 a new Central School with 24 rooms, was built on the southeast corner of Third and High streets, for grades one through eight. In 1910 a new High School was built on High Street, from Second Street west, to connect with the new Central School. Passageways on all three floors connected the new Central to the new High School, so that it was extremely difficult to tell that these were actually two buildings, constructed at different times.

Elkhart High School from the top of the Carnegie Library, in 1912, before the Municipal Building was built. The High School was designed by E. Hill Turnock.

The Elkhart High School graduating class of 1901.

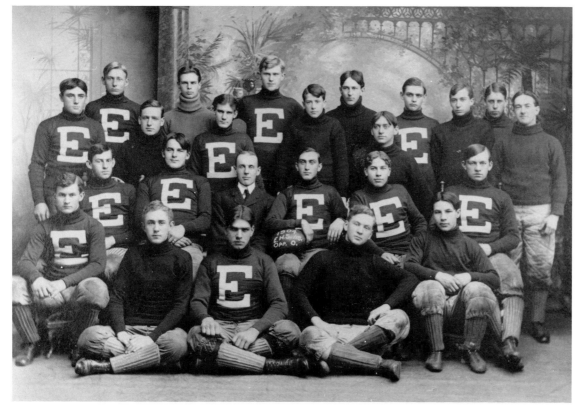

The 1904 EHS football team. That season they scored 118 points; their opponents scored zero.

In 1912 grades one through six were moved to the old high school building, which was renamed Samuel Strong School. The new Elkhart High School opened in September, 1911, having sufficient room to allow for a large increase in student enrollment. It continued to serve as Elkhart's High School for the next 60 years.

However, further expansion of the schools in Elkhart was soon needed. Willowdale Elementary (designed by E. Hill Turnock) was built in 1911, and Monger Elementary in 1915. What had been known as the new Central became officially known as Central Junior High School in 1919, accommodating grades seven through nine. Roosevelt was built to be a junior high school (as well as an elementary school) in 1921. In 1924, a gymnasium that could seat 1800, and a fine auditorium with a balcony, excellent acoustics, and a seating capacity of about 2000, were added to the High School. Prior to that year, graduation exercises and school plays were

held at the Bucklen Opera House. As a result of land being donated by James A. Rice, a local attorney, Rice Field was made available in 1923 to be used as a football stadium and for other athletic events. In 1925 Rice Elementary School was opened, and Hawthorne Elementary three years later. The concrete stadium at Rice Field, with a seating capacity of 6000, was built in 1938 by WPA workers. Wooden stadium seats, with a capacity of 4000, were built across the field, on the east side.

In 1928 when the population of Elkhart had reached about 30,000 the Vocational Annex (the only part of old Elkhart High School still standing) was built on Franklin Street, with a second floor passageway connecting it to the rest of the High School. The Annex housed the industrial education classes and shops, as well as the instrumental music and home economics departments. It was one of the first of its kind in the state of Indiana, and was the forerunner of the Elkhart

The 56 members of the January and June 1914 graduating class of Elkhart High School, on stage for their commencement exercises, at the Bucklen Opera House.

Spectators and players pose after EHS beat Nappanee 34-16 in a basketball game at the High School gym. The gymnasium in this picture preceded the "cracker-box" gym (in the same location).

141

Area Career Center, which was built in 1971 on California Road.

As early as 1940, the old "cracker box" gymnasium in the High School was overcrowded for basketball games, by fans affected by "Hoosier Hysteria." Temporary bleacher seats were added to the running track on the upper level, but by 1953, it was deemed necessary (and certainly desirable, in the thoughts of most basketball fans) to build what was, at that time, the world's largest high school gymnasium. It was built at the north end of Main Street, had a seating capacity of over 8000, and was connected to Northside Junior High School (which

also opened in the fall of 1953).

By 1949 the enrollment at Elkhart High School had reached 1079. By 1965 it had more than doubled, climbing to 2680. These great numbers caused serious consideration to be given to the idea of having two high schools in Elkhart, resulting in the construction of the Senior Division of Elkhart High School (now Elkhart Central High School), next to Rice Field, in 1966. Senior Division was originally for seniors and juniors, while Sophomore Division (formerly Elkhart High School) was only for sophomores. This plan was adopted rather than having two separate high schools — a beautiful, new building at

EHS halfback George Terlep, a star player in 1942. He later went on to play professional football in the National Football League.

The 1913 girls' basketball team, posing at one of the doorways of the new Elkhart High School.

The starting line-up, of the 1924 State Champion Blue Avalanche football team of Elkhart High School, poses with Coach Chels Boone.

142

Rice Field, and an older, less modern one in the downtown area, because the feeling at the time was that two separate high schools, located as they were, would create one school for the wealthy, and one for the less wealthy students. The new building with all its modern features quickly made it clear that the older one needed to be replaced. And so, Elkhart Memorial High School was built west of the Career Center, on California Road, in 1972.

Simply telling the story of buildings, locations, and dates leaves untouched countless memorable events and people, who made Elkhart High School what it was, and what it has become. Any listing of people and events is almost certain to leave out the "favorites" of many, but there are some individuals who must be mentioned. Mr. Sylvester B. McCracken was principal of Elkhart High School from 1892 until 1919, and a science teacher until 1933. The 1922 Pennant Annual was dedicated to him. His grave marker in Grace Lawn Cemetery was cited in *Ripley's Believe It Or Not*. It says, "School Is Out // Teacher Has Gone Home // S. B. McCracken // 1857-1933." Miss Clara Van Nuys, high school English teacher from 1890 until 1930, was also thought highly enough of by the students, that the 1924 Pennant Annual was

A picture of Erich Barnes, All-State halfback and Most Valuable Player of the 1954 EHS football team. He later played professionally in the National Football League.

> ### Elkhart High School Hymn
>
> *Oh, Elkhart High, we will be true*
> *Forever to your white and blue;*
> *And in our memories will remain*
> *The hope of coming back again*
> *To wander through familiar halls;*
> *Remembering what the heart recalls,*
> *Rememb'ring games we watched or played,*
> *And happiness in friendships made.*
> *The many lessons that we've learned*
> *The teachers for whose help we turned*
> *These are the things we shan't forget;*
> *They signify a task well met.*
> *Our school day memories hold, in truth,*
> *The joy that is the flame of youth,*
> *Dear Elkhart High, we pledge to thee*
> *Our faith, our hope, our loyalty.*

The starting five of the 1956 EHS basketball team. From left to right: Dave Kollat, free throw leader; Dick Barkman, most valuable; Max Bell, Coach of the Year; Mr. Brechler, basketball banquet speaker; Ted Luckenbill, All-State, who later played professionally in the NBA; Travis Burleson, honorary captain; and Dennis Tepe, Trester Award winner.

dedicated to her. Mr. Chelsea Boone was the legendary coach of football, basketball and track, as well as wrestling and cross country, from 1922 until 1949. His 1924 Big Blue Avalanche football team became the Indiana State Champions, with a 9-0 record, and with 414-13 as the total points scored. His 1924-25 basketball team won the Sectional and Regional, losing the first game of the State Tournament to Evansville, 20-14. His 1924 track team ended up only two points behind state champion, Kokomo. In 1933 his football team was one of the first in the country to play under the lights, introducing night football to Elkhart High School fans. The 1933 Pennant Annual was dedicated to Coach Boone.

Mr. John W. Holdeman was principal of Elkhart High School from 1922 to 1944. He was highly respected by the students, evidenced by the fact that the 1939 Pennant Annual was dedicated to him. He was affectionately referred to as "Poppa John" by many students. It was in 1930, while Mr. Holdeman was principal, that caps and gowns were first worn by graduates, to keep poorer students from feeling inferior to their richer classmates, who could afford more expensive outfits for graduation ceremonies. A third outstanding principal of Elkhart High School was Mr. C. P. Woodruff. He served in that position from 1944 to 1963, after having been an industrial arts teacher and counselor at EHS for thir-

Elkhart High School Fight Song

Fight on, Old Elkhart,
Fight for victory
With your colors flying,
We will cheer you all the way.
  Rah! Rah! Rah!
Fight on, Old Elkhart,
Fight for victory
Fight for the fame
Of our fair name.
Come on, Elkhart, win that game!
Hit 'em high,
Hit 'em low,
Go, Elkhart, Go!
Fight on, Old Elkhart,
Fight for victory
Fight for the fame
Of our fair name.
Come on, Elkhart, win that game!

Northside Gym, which was the largest high school gymnasium in the world when it was built, in 1953.

An inside view of the Northside Gym.

144

teen years. He was often called "Woody" by students and teachers alike, and had a long-standing reputation of being fair, supporting his teachers, and of listening to the concerns and needs of the students.

Three of Elkhart's superintendents each held office for eighteen years or longer. The first of these, Prof. D. W. Thomas, served from 1886 until 1906. He became prominent nationally because of his work with the National Education Association. The second superintendent, of the three, had the unusual distinction of serving as a high school English teacher for eleven years, after having served as superintendent from 1921 to 1939. Mr. J. F. Wiley (referred to by the students as "Pop" Wiley)

was well-liked by students, even though he was strict, because he showed a genuine interest in them. He was also highly respected for his knowledge of classical literature and his teaching of "higher values." Mr. Joe C. Rice was superintendent from 1949 until 1967. He presided over many changes in the Elkhart schools. These changes included opening the school board meetings to the public, as well as the press, starting the practice of hiring beginning teachers, and hiring more black teachers. There were only three black teachers in the Elkhart schools in 1949. He also ended the unwritten practice of not hiring Catholic teachers. The Elkhart School City began an extensive building program, under

The machine shop in the new EHS Vocational Annex, in 1928.

"Mr. B," the Elkhart Blue Blazer mascot, designed in 1955 by Mr. Howard James, EHS art teacher.

The victorious State Runner-up EHS basketball team, returning to a big celebration in Elkhart, in 1971.

Mr. Rice, to meet the expansion demands of over 100% increases in enrollment. The Educational Services Center of the Elkhart Community Schools (west of Memorial High School) has been named in honor of Mr. Rice.

Two teachers, whose careers at Elkhart High School paralleled each other, will certainly live forever in the memories of nearly every student who attended EHS, from the mid-1920's to the early 1960's. Miss Dorothy Kelly, long-time sponsor and "guiding light" of the High School publications, the Pennant Weekly and the Pennant Annual, was an English teacher from 1926 until 1966. She is remembered for the high standards she demanded of her students, and the high level of preparation she gave them. After going off to college, many of her students found that they were far better prepared than their less fortunate classmates from other high schools. Mr. Ivan Gill was another master teacher who demanded high standards of his students. He taught chemistry from 1923 until 1959. Like Miss Kelly, Mr. Gill was truly a legend in his time, filling students with respect and awe, and teaching higher values, in addition to the academic subject matter. Certainly there have been many other outstanding master teachers at Elkhart High School, as well as at the elementary and

The auto shop in the EHS Vocational Annex, in 1928.

A driver's training car in the 1950's. Football coach John Janzaruk, driver education teacher, can be seen in the front seat.

Students line up to buy tickets, at the athletic ticket office inside the door at EHS, in the 1940's.

junior high schools, but restrictions of time and space preclude mentioning many who deserve this recognition.

In 1949 Elkhart High School was one of the first high schools in the nation to have exchange students (students from other countries) enroll for a school year, while living in the homes of EHS students, as their "brothers" and "sisters." The honor of being the youngest graduate of Elkhart High School goes to a fourteen year old black student, Leonard W. Johnson, Jr. He graduated in 1947, went to Howard University Medical School, and later became a high-ranking officer in the United States Air Force. The first black student to grad-

uate from EHS was Aletha Hoosier, in 1925. Other outstanding black graduates include: Tom Atkins (President of the Student Council in 1957), who later became President of the student body at Indiana University, and then a successful politician in Massachusetts; Erich Barnes, Shafer Suggs, and Ernie Jones, all of whom became professional football players in the National Football League; and Charles Gordone, a Pulitzer prize-winning playwright.

There have been many noteworthy athletic teams at Elkhart High School. They include Coach Tom Kurth's 1968 Blue Blazer football team, which had a perfect 10-0

The windows over the front door of EHS, seen from the third floor hall, outside the balcony doors to the auditorium.

The Elkhart High School marching band forming an "E," at Rice Field in 1942. There are four Sousaphones in the front row.

record, and was rated first in the state. Also, in 1968, the EHS wrestling team, under Coach Rollie Hoover, won the state championship. That same year, Coach Jim Eger's track team won the state championship as well. Marshall McCullough,who was a junior that year, became the only EHS athlete to be on three state championship teams. He starred on the football, wrestling, and track teams in 1968-69.

Coach Bill Milliner's basketball team made it to the Final Four in the State Basketball Tourney in 1954, but lost the first game. This feat was repeated

in 1956. The very best showing for an EHS basketball team came under the leadership of Coach Keith Dougherty, in 1971. The Blue Blazers advanced to the final game of the State Tournament for the first time in history. Even though they were finally defeated 70-60, they were officially the number two team in the state.

Memories of Elkhart High School would not be complete, without including the music department. Both the EHS band and orchestra began in 1922, with Mr. J. C. Cheney as Director. In 1933, under the direc-

Mr. S. B. McCracken, in 1922.

Miss Clara Van Nuys, in 1924.

Mr. J. F. Wiley, in 1933.

Coach Chelsea C. Boone, in 1933.

tion of Mr. David Hughes, the EHS orchestra won the State Band and Orchestra Contest, and in 1937, they won the First Division in the National Contest at Columbus, Ohio. In 1952 Mr. John Davies took over the reins as Director of the Elkhart High School Band and Orchestra, and worked tirelessly to develop an outstanding instrumental music program, enriching the lives of many EHS students. During his time as director, in 1957-58, EHS students won a total of 158 gold medals at the State Solo and Ensemble Contest in Indianapolis, breaking the state record of 128 gold medals for students at one school. One other important musical figure at Elkhart High School was Choir Director William Gowdy. For many years, one of the musical highlights of the school year was the annual Christmas Choir Concert, featuring a human Christmas tree. The tree was made of choir students holding pine branches and candle-shaped flashlights. The student who sold the most tickets to the concert was given the honor of being at the very top of the Christmas tree.

Mr. John W. Holdeman, in 1942.

Mr. C. P. Woodruff, in 1954.

Mr. Ivan C. Gill, in 1949.

Miss Dorothy Kelly, in 1949.

Lew Bowen and his son, Frank, are shown here, in front of
their Mobil service station on the southwest corner of Bower
and Michigan Streets, about 1949.

Fisher's Standard Service, at Lexington and Vistula, is seen
here in 1942. This gas station is located across the intersection from Samuel Strong School.

Taken in 1947, this picture shows Harold's Mobil service
station, on the southeast corner of Third and Lexington,
with the familiar "flying horse" emblem.

This is the Lincoln Auto Garage, in 1916, at 1328 South
Main Street. Standing in front of the garage are (left to
right): Floyd Hamlet, Harry Hime, Leon Stover (barefooted),
and Harry Stover (the owner).

This is what the interior of one of Lloyd's grocery stores looked like, about 1933. This store was located in the 500 block of South Main Street.

The inside of Cuppy's cigar store, at 411 South Main Street, about 1914.

Oliver Harvey, driver of the delivery wagon, is waiting in front of the J. G. Klein grocery store, about 1893. The store was located at 111 West Pigeon Street (Lexington).

In 1958 one visionary speculated that Main Street might look like this twenty years in the future (1978). First National Bank is the second building from the right (on the southwest corner of Main and High Streets).

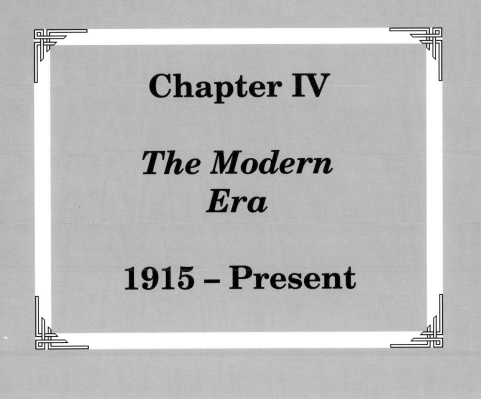

Chapter IV

The Modern Era

1915 – Present

The last 75 years have been a time of great change in Elkhart, as well as the rest of the world. The population of the city more than doubled. Local soldiers fought and died in World War I, the returning troops being greeted with great celebrations. Citizens of Elkhart experienced the 20's and 30's in much the same way as the rest of the nation. In Elkhart there were Chautauquas in the park, and dance bands at the Atherton Club and the Athenian Room. In addition, there was the new Lerner Theater (now the Elco), and the new Hotel Elkhart. There was Prohibition, and the Great Depression with its WPA workers. Streetcars passed from the scene and were replaced by city busses, which in turn were replaced by privately-owned automobiles as the principal means of transportation.

While World War II pulled Elkhart, as well as the rest of the nation, out of the Great Depression, it also brought new difficulties. Gold Star Mothers displayed signs of their sons' heroism and sacrifice. Everyone experienced the frustrations of food and gasoline rationing. In classrooms, school children bought postal savings stamps. The dimes and quarters spent on these stamps eventually bought United States Savings Bonds, which helped the war effort. Air Raid Wardens patrolled the streets during blackouts, and soldiers were given the privilege of boarding trains before civilians.

Milk was delivered to customers' doors, and if it was not brought in soon enough on cold winter mornings, the cream would push upward, tilting the bottle caps. Many people still used ice boxes, instead of refrigerators. Twice each week they would display cards in their windows, indicating how many pounds of ice they needed. On hot summer days, young children followed the ice man as he went about his route. When the ice man stopped his truck and carried cakes of ice to people's houses, the children would "steal" small pieces of ice that had been chipped off, and enjoy the refreshing treat.

Over the years, culture in Elkhart flourished, as the Municipal Band, the Elkhart Symphony Orchestra, the Academy of Ballet Arts, with its Ballet Etudes (a teenage performing group), the Civic Theatre, and (later) the Warren School of Ballet and the Michiana Ballet Company all developed. Also the Concert Club brought nationally-famous performing artists to town. Connie Sykes, long active in the music scene in Elkhart, and organist for the Christian Science Church for 50 years, delighted many audiences at Kiwanis travelogues with her unforgettable organ playing before each show. The Centennial cele-

bration in 1958 was a major event, with a director brought from New York to coordinate a special show at Rice Field. The Centennial celebration involved countless residents of Elkhart in a wide variety of festive activities.

During this period, Elkhart experienced some "natural" disasters. There were several floods, and the Palm Sunday tornados which etched their deadly paths through the countryside, and through the lives and minds of nearly everyone who lived in the area. The great blizzard of 1978 and the drought of 1988 served as vivid reminders of how good it is to be able to turn to our neighbors in times of need. The band instrument business in Elkhart diminished noticeably in size and importance when Conn's moved away, but the gap was already being filled by Schult, Skyline, Richardson, and many others in the recreational vehicle and mobile home business, both in Elkhart and in the rest of the county.

Many old landmarks are gone now: Elkhart High School, with its auditorium and "cracker-box" gym, Carnegie Library, the Trinity Methodist, Christian Science, First Baptist, and domed Presbyterian downtown churches, the YMCA, Monger Building, Century Club, old Miles building, Hotel Bucklen, and the Bucklen Opera House all are gone. Only memories are left of the A & W Root Beer Barrels, steam locomotives, roundhouses, and of the Main Street crossing gate booth.

However, in this era, Elkhart has put on a new face, with the Ameritrust National Bank complex, the Civic Plaza and Midway Motor Lodge, new telephone, electric, and gas company buildings, the county courts building, and the NBD Midwest Commerce Bank building. In addition, there are other new banks, as well as new police and fire department buildings, a new library, and a new post office. The schools have expanded, adding Northside, Pierre Moran, Westside (and for awhile Brookdale) junior high schools, as well as Central High School, Memorial High School, the Career Center, and of course, the Northside Gym. Purdue University, I.U.S.B., and Ivy Tech have all established extensions in Elkhart.

Numerous parking lots have appeared in the downtown area, also a McDonald's, a Dairy Queen, and the underpass. The Nappanee Street extension, a larger airport, the Toll Road, the Pierre Moran and Concord malls have all been added on the borders of the city. While Elkhart is no longer "what it used to be," the city and its citizens continue to handle the challenges, and move forward.

Winnie Shelt's newsstand was located at the corner of Main and Tyler, near the railroad tracks, from 1914 until he retired in 1959. The newsstand was donated by the police and fire departments, as well as by other citizens, in 1947. It was open from 5 a.m. to 7 p.m. seven days a week.

Laurie Broderick, who graduated with honors from Elkhart Memorial High School, became Miss Elkhart County in 1985, and was crowned Miss Indiana the same year. In the Miss America Pageant, Laurie became a preliminary talent winner, and was selected as a top ten semi-finalist. She also won the United States Grand National Twirling Championship, in 1982.

WORLD WAR I

Thomas McCoy, first Elkhart boy to give his life for his country in World War I. He died in France on February 23, 1918. The Elkhart American Legion post was named after him.

A group of Elkhart Volunteers ready to board the train for basic training, and their participation in the war effort.

Troops occupying Island Park during Wold War I (Battery E Headquarters, Indiana State Militia).

Elkhart Red Cross
Canteen workers out-
side the New York
Central Railroad
depot in 1918.

Elkhart celebrates
the homecoming of
Battery E, January
15, 1919. This view
is looking north,
from the 500 block
of South Main
Street.

Sergeant Arthur O.
Johnson, one of the
last Elkhart soldiers
to die in World War I.

PARKS

Within the city limits, Elkhart has an abundance of parks. Some of the parks are small; some better known than others. One very popular park around the turn of the century, was a privately-owned business. In 1894 Samuel E. Barney paid $13,000 for the land which is now occupied by the Christiana Creek Country Club, at the north end of Main Street. He brought in clay from the West, and hired an architect from Chicago to design a clubhouse. By 1896 the one-mile Racing Park was open for business. Many varied events took place for about thirty years, including sulky races and horse races, even a race between Barney Oldfield in his motor race car and Lincoln Beachey in his biplane (in 1914). The Elkhart High School athletic department made use of this area for a variety of sports until Rice Field became available in 1924.

Charles Beardsley (grandson of Havilah), sold Island Park to the city in 1881 for $200. Studebaker Park was given to the city of Elkhart by Peter E. and John M. Studebaker (of South Bend) in 1889, on the condition that the city maintain it as a park forever. High Dive Park was developed by Charlie Fieldhouse, and later sold to the city. It was opened to the public in 1941, and stirs up memories of "the old swimmin' hole" to thousands who have enjoyed it as a place to cool off on a hot summer day. One of the smallest, more recently opened parks, is Lundquist Bicentennial Park. Dedicated on July 4, 1977, it is connected to

About 1905, Fred H. Davis, skipper of the excursion boat "Chautauqua," ties up at the McNaughton park dock.

A pleasant afternoon outing at Island park, around the beginning of the twentieth century.

160

Island Park by a footbridge, and is named after Eldy Lundquist, a former local sportscaster and state representative.

When the Highland Park residential addition to the city was laid out in 1887, the area along the river was designated as a park, but remained the private property of the Elkhart Real Estate Association until John McNaughton acquired it for $3000 in 1905. He gave it to the city with the understanding that it be named McNaughton Park, and be the site of a "Chautauqua" for at least five years. A Chautauqua is patterned after the Chautauqua Institution in New York, which includes lectures, musical and dance events, brief foreign language courses, scientific demonstrations, and various kinds of seminars, usually held outdoors under tents. Among the well-known speakers at Elkhart Chautauquas were William Jennings Bryan, Billy Sunday, Carrie Nation, Booker T. Washington, and Mrs. LaSalle Pickett (wife of the Confederate general). The varied assemblies were held yearly at McNaughton Park until 1917. A break occurred in 1918, due to World War I. The assemblies resumed in 1919, but at Island Park continuing until 1932. Single admission from 1907 to 1912 was twelve cents, with season tickets costing $2.00. People attending from farther away rented tents during their stay. The Elkhart Municipal Band held summertime concerts on Island Park for many years, later moving to McNaughton Park, where a permanent band shell was erected, and the summer concert series continues.

The High Dive swimming pool, located north of East Beardsley Avenue and west of Johnson Street, opened in 1941.

A close-up of the High Dive diving boards.

A 175-foot toboggan slide at the High Dive.

The old windmill at the High Dive.

A picture of Miss Knell's class in basket weaving. This was one of the many activities held at an Elkhart Chautauqua at McNaughton Park, about 1910.

Kryl's band performing at a Chautauqua in McNaughton Park.

The assembly tent at a Chautauqua in McNaughton Park, about 1910.

These seven automobile owners got together at McNaughton Park in 1908 to organize the distribution of Chautauqua literature. Included in this picture are: J. W. Fieldhouse, A. H. Beardsley, R. R. Beardsley, and R. C. Barney.

Pausing in their festivities, this group at a McNaughton Park Chautauqua poses for a picture.

The playgrounds at McNaughton Park (at a Chautauqua) were used extensively.

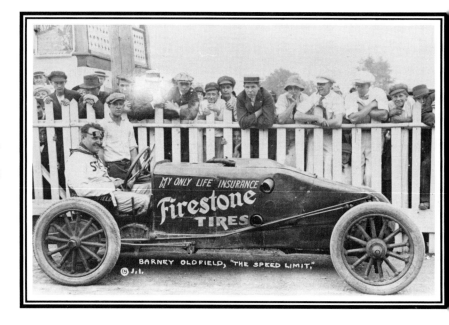

Barney Oldfield, ready to begin a race, about 1912 at the Elkhart Driving Park.

Lincoln Beachey at the controls of his biplane, in 1912 at the Elkhart Driving Park.

Barney Oldfield (in his motor race car) racing with Lincoln Beachey (in his biplane) at the Elkhart Driving Park in 1912. Beachey won.

Glenn H. Curtiss (pilot) and his famous evangelist passenger, Billy Sunday, arriving at Winona Lake. They are on their way to a Chautauqua in Elkhart.

Evangelist Billy Sunday addresses a crowd in the assembly tent at the Elkhart Chautauqua in McNaughton Park. The year is 1913.

The crowd seems ready for excitement at the Elkhart Driving Park. The Walley ambulance is ready, too.

A sulky race at the Old Elkhart Driving Park. The park was located at the northeast corner of Middlebury Street and Simpson Avenue.

These five chartered Elkhart city busses are lined up (in 1949), in front of the High School Annex on West Franklin Street.

The first hangar was constructed at the Elkhart airport in 1940. A flagpole was donated by Dr. Swihart to the Elkhart Flying Service, and some gasoline pumps were installed. Various other improvements were made after that time, including the paving of a 2600-foot east-west runway in 1955. The ownership of the airport was transferred to the City of Elkhart, four years later.

The first taxi cab service in Elkhart was offered by the Hotel Bucklen, and began in 1910. Glen Miller was the first cab driver, and used a 1910 two-cylinder Buick touring car. He was the father of Elkhart movie theater owner, William Miller. In the 1920's, the Yellow Cab Company operated from the Hotel Elkhart. In those days, a cab would take a passenger anywhere in town for a quarter. The Ace Cab Company was started by Robert T. Personett in 1947, in the basement of the Hotel Bucklen. Fifteen years later, it moved to its present location at 300 East High Street. The Ace taxi shown in this picture is a 1949 Plymouth.

This is an aerial view of downtown Elkhart, taken about 1948, looking north from Tyler Avenue.

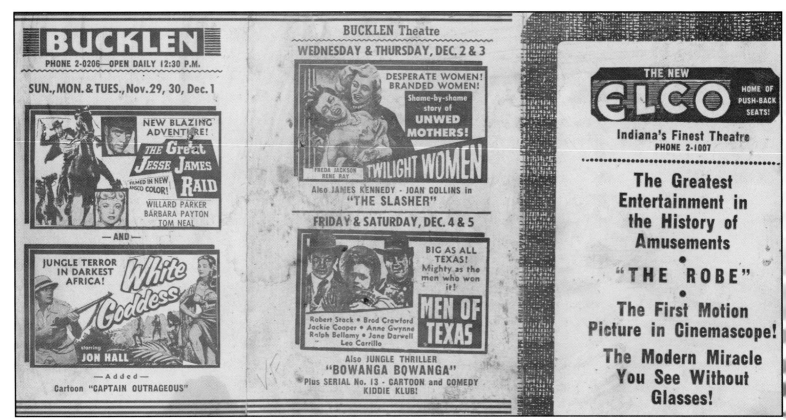

An advertising flyer from the Elkhart movie theaters. These flyers were available at the Elco, Orpheum, and Bucklen theaters in the 1950's, and told what movies would be showing at each theater during the coming week. In those days, a movie usually showed for no more than four days. Normally a cartoon, a newsreel, and sometimes another short feature were included. Cinemascope was brought to the Elco with the movie, "The Robe." This was before television was in very many homes.

A picture of the entrance to the Family Theater, at 421 South Main Street, about 1915. The Family Theater was in business only from 1914 to 1925. The building later housed the Singer Sewing Machine store. After a fire, this building was demolished, and is now the site of a parking lot. Other movie theaters which were open only a few years were: the Crystal, the Globe, the Bijou, the Princess, the Royal, the Star, the Majestic, the Venetian, the Hippodrome, the Rex, the Lyric, the Peter Pan, the Subway, and the Ban Box. The State Theater, which is still operating, opened in 1939.

The Orpheum Theater, which opened on Thanksgiving Day in 1913, was located at 210 South Main Street. After many years, it was bought by Bill Miller, who remodeled it inside and out, and renamed it Cinema I. It is still standing.

The Lerner Theater was dedicated on Thanksgiving Day in 1924. In 1933, under new management, the name of the theater was changed to the Elco. In this picture, a large crowd is posing before the beginning of a show on Mothers' Day, May, 1948.

DANCE ORCHESTRAS IN ELKHART

The Atherton Orchestra, shown here in 1914, provided "unexcelled music" for dances, banquets, and receptions at the Atherton Club, a popular social organization that met in the old Century Club building at 115 North Main Street. J. Dusek directed the orchestra.

In 1917 Steimrich's Orchestra was very popular in Elkhart. It featured Homer Spicer on the trombone, Harvey Lewis on the clarinet, Orland Banning on the drums, Albert Steimer at the piano, and Cleo Ulrich on the saxophone. According to the advertisements, they played "dance music that tickles your feet."

This picture, taken on July 13, 1904, is of the YMCA "Symphony" Orchestra.

In 1898 the Trumpet Notes band met the soldiers of Company E. at the Big Four railroad station to welcome them home from the Spanish-American War. The C. G. Conn Trumpet Notes Band was Elkhart's leading band for 31 years. The Willis Band (another local band) joined with the Trumpet Notes in 1915. This band later became known as the Elkhart Municipal Band.

Franc Erb and his orchestra are seen here at the Elks Club on South Main Street in 1928. They played songs such as "Five-Foot-Two," "That Old Gang Of Mine," "Tiger Rag," and "Ain't She Sweet?" This group was active from 1926 until about 1931, playing locally, and as far away as Goshen and Sturgis. Shown (from left to right) are: Russell Hager, Howard Baumgartner, Reggie Andrews, Russell Calkins, Ed Streeter, Francis Erb (at the piano), and Chet Yeazel. Vocalist Harold Fulkerson is standing behind Ed Streeter.

The Pharmanette, in 1924, on the southwest corner of Main and Franklin.

Roger Kendall brought joy to the hearts of many, especially children, who learned to regard this policeman as a friend. He played Santa Claus for many years, visiting countless children in schools and in the hospital. He was known as "the whistling policeman."

During World War II, all possible efforts were made to conserve scarce resources on the "home front." Food and fuel were rationed, and (as shown in this picture in 1942) scrap metal was collected for the war effort. This Official U. S. Salvage Depot was across the street from the police and fire station, on East Franklin Street. The building on the right is Paxon's feed store.

These salvage trucks are gathered on the east side of the central fire station, on East Franklin Street (in 1942), to help with scrap metal collection, as a part of the war effort. East Street and Waterfall Drive are visible at the top of the picture.

DISASTERS

A fire at the H. B. Sykes dry goods store, in the winter of 1904, drew a large number of spectators, in spite of the wintery weather. The dry goods store was located on the northwest corner of Main and High streets, and later became Drake's department store.

The Harvest Queen flour mill was built on the northeast corner of Elkhart Avenue and East Jackson Boulevard in 1869. It was owned by the Sage brothers. The mill burned down in 1909, as shown in this picture.

In many ways, the Blizzard of 1978 was a record-setter. A total of 22 inches of snow fell from January 25 through January 27. Fourteen inches fell on the 26th, which was a record for one day. The total snowfall for the month was 36.6 inches, another record. The snow, combined with gale-force winds much of that time, caused high drifts which reached the rooftops of many homes. Policemen, paramedics, and other emergency personnel had to use snowmobiles to reach people in need. Almost all normal activity came to a stop, with more than 10,000 workers being idled, while the digging-out efforts were carried on. Many people in the surrounding countryside were snowed in for a week.

The greatest local disaster occurred on April 11, 1965, when twin tornados hit Elkhart and its surrounding area. Fifty-two people were killed in Elkhart County alone. Other twisters passed through Indiana that day killing 58 more. Total property damage amounted to over $100 million. On that Palm Sunday, around 6:00 p.m., photographer Paul Huffman of the *Elkhart Truth,* was nearing Dunlap (coming from Goshen) on US 33, when he saw some ominous black clouds approaching. Jumping out of his car to take a picture, he saw the clouds form into two funnels, hit the Midway Trailer Court, and then swerve away from the road, narrowly missing him. The picture shown here is one he took that day. It has since won many awards, and in 1985 was featured in an exhibit at Elkhart's Midwest Museum of Art.

Rice Field looked like a very large swimming pool, when the Elkhart River flooded in 1950.

BANKS

First Old State Bank (not to be confused with First State Bank) was founded in 1920. It was located on the west side of the 400 block of South Main Street. In 1952 this bank had the distinction of being the first to open a downtown drive-in facility. First Old State Bank merged with St. Joseph Valley Bank in 1966.

St. Joseph Valley Bank was established in 1872 at 119 South Main Street. It moved to the Cornish building on the southwest corner of Main and Lexington in 1889, and to the Security building at 214 South Main in 1904. After merging with First State Bank, the St. Joe Valley Bank moved again, to the southwest corner of Main and Franklin, in 1915. The building in this picture was built by the St. Joseph Valley Bank in 1922, on the northwest corner of Main and Marion, and after moving into it, the bank remained there for 52 years. In 1974 a move was made to the southeast corner of Franklin and Second. The old building became the Midwest Museum of Art. When eight years later, the St. Joseph Valley Bank merged with the First National Bank of Goshen, it changed its name to Midwest Commerce Banking Company. In 1986 NBD Bancorp (National Bank of Detroit) bought the Midwest Commerce Banking Company.

Looking north on Main Street, from the corner of Tyler Avenue, in 1957. At this time, Main Street was one-way headed north. Second Street was one-way headed south. Merchants on Main Street complained that this arrangement discouraged the traffic coming through town on U.S. 20 (Jackson Boulevard) from driving past their places of business, because cars could not turn on South Main Street from Jackson. As a result of their objections, Main Street was changed back to a two-way street, and Second was made one-way headed north. Third Street was made one way headed south.

The famous (or infamous) Arch of Elkhart which spanned the corner of Main and Franklin streets from 1963 to 1968. Looking north in 1967, this picture shows the arch doing what it was originally intended to do—support a large municipal Christmas tree. Over the years, it supported other things as well, such as a United Fund poster, a tall flag pole, and a small mobile home. In 1968 it was dismantled, and part of it was used to construct the overhead walkway, near the west end of Strong Avenue, from Mary Daly School, across Nappanee Street to West Side Junior High School.

MEMOIRS

The first McDonald's restaurant in Elkhart was built in 1960 on the southeast corner of Main and Jefferson streets. It is still there, but the hamburgers cost more than fifteen cents today.

This picture, taken in the mid-1950's, shows Elkhart's first laundromat. The building was on the north side of East Jackson, near Main Street, having been originally used in the 1880's as the horse and trolley barn.

The River Queen, Elkhart's stern-wheeler riverboat, was built about 1950 by Robert "Red" Macumber and his brother, William. It was later enlarged. Many groups have enjoyed an old-fashioned ride up and down the "St. Joe" on the River Queen, and from its top deck, the Elkhart Symphony Orchestra has serenaded boaters, as well as riverside residents. The River Queen has been in dry dock since 1988.

The old A & W Root Beer Barrel, at the southeast corner of Main and Sycamore streets. It was located one block from the bridge to Island park, and was the scene where many thirsts were quenched over the years. A frosty mug of A & W Root Beer really hit the spot on a hot summer day! This was only one of six such root beer barrels in Elkhart in the 1950s.

Opening day for the Elkhart Dairy Queen at 109 South Second Street (March 16, 1962) did not bring the crowds that appeared later with the onset of warmer weather. The D-X gas station in the background was on the southwest corner of Second and Jackson.

"Slim," the manager of the Dairy Queen, is shown here in 1958, on one of his "Good Humor" vehicles.

Ralph Murphy, known as "Murph, the whistling milkman," began his job with Grady Dairy in the summer of 1941. After serving 38 months in the U.S. Army during World War II, he resumed delivering milk to his customers, who thought of him as a friend. He is shown here with his faithful horse, Tony, in 1953, the last year horse-drawn milk wagons were used for home delivery. Beside him is Lowell Metzler, and his motorized milk truck, an indication of the change to come.

BALLET

The second floor of the Bucklen Opera House was the site where ballet and ballet history were studied. The teacher, Nadine Thornton, is shown here (about 1957), giving budding ballerinas an understanding of ballet history in relation to changing times and conditions. Clockwise from the teacher are: Shirley Hoffman, Martha Starr, Paula Culp, Susan Sherman, Maija Baltpurvins, Betty Grillo, and Pamela Davis.

This is a scene from the ballet, "Festival at Straussburg." The dancers (from left to right) are: Kathryn Hull, Jacque Fields, Pamela Green, Sandra Abplanalp, Paula Culp, Shirley Hoffman, Susan Sherman, Carol Warfel, Martha Starr, and Maija Baltpurvins. This ballet was choreographed by Nadine Thornton, the director of the Academy of Ballet Arts, in Elkhart. The music was by Johann Strauss, Jr. Many ballet classes and rehearsals took place in spacious rooms on the second floor of the Bucklen Opera House. This ballet was performed at the Elkhart High School auditorium, in April of 1958.

THE ARTS

Few people realize that a little girl named Mary Tomlinson, who moved to Elkhart with her family in 1899 (at the age of nine), grew up to become a well-known movie star. Her father, the Reverend Samuel J. Tomlinson, was pastor of First Christian Church (now Central Christian Church), and the family lived at 109 West Washington Street. In 1901 the family moved to Shelbyville, Indiana. Mary acted in more than 80 Hollywood films, and won an Academy Award nomination (in 1947) for her role as Ma Kettle in the movie "The Egg And I." While travelling with a Shakespearean company, she met her future husband, Dr. Stanley LeFevre Krebs, a lecturer on the Chautauqua circuit. He gave her the stage name—Marjorie Main. She co-starred with Percy Kilbride in nine other "Ma and Pa Kettle" films.

Jean Hagen, another Elkhart girl, got her start as an actress on the radio. Later she starred in Broadway shows and in Hollywood movies with Robert Taylor, Jimmy Stewart, Spencer Tracy, and Katherine Hepburn. Still later, she played Danny Thomas' wife on the television show, "Make Room For Daddy," for which she received two Emmy nominations. She graduated from Elkhart High School as Jean Verhagen in 1941.

The Elkhart Symphony Orchestra began in 1948, under the direction of Zigmont G. Gaska. Michael Esselstrom is the second and present conductor.

The first Elkhart Municipal Band concert was held on July 4, 1938, at Rice Field, preceding the fireworks show. The first conductor was Milburn McKay.

SPORTS

One of the early baseball teams in Elkhart was called the Sidway Colts. Their clubhouse was on Eighth Street, between Garfield and Cleveland. The players (from left to right) are: Top row: Bishop, Eash, Groves, and Beaver; Middle row: unknown, Statton, unknown, and unknown; Bottom row: Dan Eash and Jess Ruff.

Elkhart's first black baseball team was called the Giants. They played for about three years in the early 1930's. In the front row (left to right) are: Otis "Bill" Stamper, "Son" Hansborough, Clint Stamper, Jim Bell, Carnel Flowers, and Ramon "Puerto Rico" Santiago. In the back row are: Jesse Curry (umpire), Willie Bonds, Ed Gamble, Riley McGee, Fred Ballard, and Herbert Campbell.

The new concrete stadium at Rice Field was completed in time for the 1939 football season. The construction, which cost $120,000 was done by WPA workers. The cinder track around the football field was built to Big Ten college specifications.

RICE ATHLETIC FIELD
OF ELKHART HIGH SCHOOL,
SHOWING ELKHART RIVER,
ELKHART, IND.—32

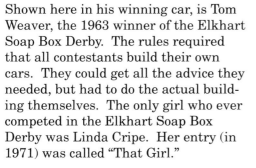

In this picture, which was taken in 1960, Roger Sevison is shown winning the Elkhart Soap Box Derby. The Derby was held each year, from 1948 to 1971, at McNaughton Park. The winner competed at the National Soap Box Derby in Akron, Ohio.

Shown here in his winning car, is Tom Weaver, the 1963 winner of the Elkhart Soap Box Derby. The rules required that all contestants build their own cars. They could get all the advice they needed, but had to do the actual building themselves. The only girl who ever competed in the Elkhart Soap Box Derby was Linda Cripe. Her entry (in 1971) was called "That Girl."

Eldy Lundquist is remembered for his broadcasts of Elkhart High School basketball and football games. His description of the action made the listeners feel as if they were actually present at the games. Later he was elected as Elkhart's state representative to the Indiana General Assembly.

This picture, showing the bowling lanes at the Red Crown Bowling Alley, was taken in 1956. The building had previously housed the Bucklen Livery, and was located at 117 East Lexington Avenue.

This tobbogan slide, built in 1887, was near Vistula Street, in the area called "the Flats." Because the tobbogan fad was sweeping the country, the builders hoped to make a fortune, charging five cents per ride. The best night brought in $120, which meant a total of 2400 rides! However, in 1887 and 1888, early thaws ended the winter season prematurely, causing the owners to sell the tobbogans and tear down the slide. There were several other elaborate slides built in Elkhart during 1888 and 1891, but they fared no better, due to uncooperative weather and waning public interest.

ELKHART CENTENNIAL ===

Local theater owner, William P. Miller, was active in civic affairs for many years. In 1958 he was the General Chairman for the Elkhart Centennial Committee.

The Grand Marshal of the Elkhart Centennial Parade in 1958 was Mrs. Ida Eller. She was born on February 6, 1858, and moved to Elkhart as a small child. At first, her family lived in a log cabin on Johnson Street, and at that time there were still Indians in the area. One of her earliest memories was of her stepfather leaving for the Civil War, only two hours after marrying her mother.

Julie Yeknik, Miss Elkhart Centennial, and the members of her court, are shown here on the 1958 Elkhart Centennial Parade float.

The Elkhart Institute of Technology began as a business college, in 1882. It was first located on the second floor of 208 South Main Street, and then moved to a number of other sites, including the Monger Building. The name of the school was changed over the years. It was known as the Elkhart Business College, and as the Elkhart University of Medical and Dental Technology. By 1965 the school had an enrollment of 525 students, and occupied parts of three buildings. Three years later, it was sold to a Chicago firm, which operated it until its closing in 1987. This picture shows the school when it was located at 516 South Main (the former Odd Fellows building).

The Elkhart Area Career Center, known far and wide as one of the best area vocational schools, was built on California Road in 1971.

Elkhart Memorial High School was built in 1972, directly
west of the Career Center on California Road.

Elkhart Central High School was originally called Senior Division
(of Elkhart High School). It was built in 1966 next to Rice Field.

AMERITRUST NATIONAL BANK

The foundation of Ameritrust National Bank, Michiana was laid in 1842 when Philo Morehous, under the Free Banking law, opened the Bank of Elkhart. The first facility was located in the Morehous store.

The Bank of Elkhart continued under the management of its founder until 1863, when a charter was issued under the National Banking Act which created the First National Bank of Elkhart. The First National Bank of Elkhart was among the first chartered by the Government, being number 206.

The bank then moved to a corner room of the Clifton House. One of the first "big" transactions was the purchase of $25,000 in U.S. Bonds when the war distressed government was desperately in need of funds. This was less than six weeks after the bank opened for business under its national charter.

Since the turn of the century there have been many changes in the physical structure and facilities of the bank. In 1918 the bank moved into a new building at its present location at the corner of Main and High Streets. In 1925 these quarters were doubled,

and in 1936 the building was remodeled to provide greater customer space.

In 1954 the bank purchased the former S.S. Kresge Company at 303 South Main Street and constructed the original three story building.

In 1977, First National Bank acquired the Penney and McClellan buildings and began another major renovation. The McClellan building was demolished and additional parking space was created. The Penney building was remodeled to provide 25,000 square feet of additional office space.

The most recent renovation was completed in 1988 with 47,000 square feet of additional office space. Throughout the years and the remodeling process, the projects were completed without an interruption of banking service.

On May 30, 1986, shareholders of First National Bank approved the merger with Ameritrust Corporation, Cleveland. On June 5, 1989, the bank changed its name from First National Bank, Elkhart to Ameritrust National Bank, Michiana. Today total assets of the holding company are over $11 billion.

Philo Morehous. Founder and first president.

The Clifton House. The second location of First National Bank

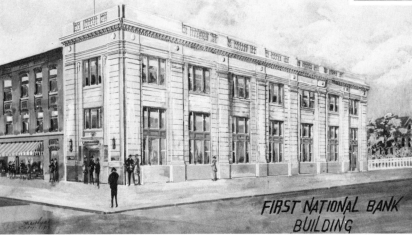

FIRST NATIONAL BANK BUILDING

Original building of First National Bank on the corner of Main and High Streets.

Early bank lobby. The fourth man from the left, in the background, is Charles H. Winchester, President of First National from 1887 – 1917.

Before the 1977 remodeling showing the J.C. Penney building.

The bank's lobby also underwent changes in 1980.

This photo shows the bank after major renovation in 1980.

BEFORE AND AFTER...

This aerial view of Elkhart, taken in the mid-1960's, shows much of the same area as the photo below.

An aerial sketch of Elkhart in 1874 shows the Elkhart River entering the St. Joseph River through two channels, instead of one, creating some additional islands. The area at the top right, showing a number of channels, or raceways, was called "the hydraulics." The raceways provided water power to operate mills and factories. This area is now known as Easy Shopping Place. At the far left, the trees and grassy area, which are now West Jefferson and Sherman streets, were then used as the town cow pasture. On the northwest corner of Main and Harrison, a block north of the railroad tracks in the lower right corner of this picture, a small tavern or inn owned by Eli and Mary Hilton is shown occupying the site where the Bucklen Opera House was built ten years later. At the far left top of this picture is Benjamin Davenport's home and the Main Street bridge.

RV Industry

This building, located at 515 Harrison Street, was Elkhart's first trailer factory. Wilbur J. Schult began operations here in 1935, employing 20 carpenters. The factory produced one trailer per day, and each trailer was sold for $198. This building was torn down in 1957.

In 1936 Schult moved his operations to this building, the former Noyes Carriage Company, which was built in 1897 on South Main Street. Schult produced 1000 trailers that year.

This 1937 Schult trailer was advertised as "the latest in travelling comfort." It is a 12-foot Sport trailer. The Schult Trailer Company turned out 1500 units in 1937, at that time making it one of the top trailer producers in the nation.

This picture shows an aerial view of the Indiana Mobile Home Association's annual mobile home show, which was held at the Northside Gym in 1959. The show grew larger each year, and after 1968, had to be held at the Notre Dame A.C.C. Schult was the first producer of trailers in Indiana, but by 1969, there were more than 80 mobile home manufacturers in the Elkhart area alone. Such companies as Skyline, Richardson, Coachmen, and many others have given Elkhart and Elkhart County a reputation of being the Mobile Home and Recreational Vehicle Capital of the World.

193

The east side of the 300 block of South Main Street in 1976, two years before these buildings were demolished and the Midway Motor Lodge was built.

Looking south on Main Street in the late 1960s, from north of the corner of Main and Lexington. "Gone With the Wind" was playing (once again) at the Orpheum theater.

This picture shows the County Courts building, which was built on the north-west corner of Second and Franklin streets. It was built in order to meet the expanding needs of county government. The building was dedicated in December of 1971.

The Security building, at 214 South Main Street, is one of the more unusual examples of architecture in Elkhart. The front of the building is made of red sandstone, while the rest of it is made of brick. Built in 1892, it has housed banks, law offices, and a variety of other businesses. This picture was taken in 1989. Cinema I (a movie theater) can be seen on the left.

Located at 311 West High Street and for many years known as the Four Arts Club, this was original-ly the home of Albert R. and Elizabeth Baldwin Beardsley. This house was a wedding gift from her father Silas Baldwin, and it was from here that Elizabeth and Albert planned and built Ruthmere. Over the years, many cultural events, such as recitals, book reviews, and musi-cal programs have been held in this home.

ACKNOWLEDGMENTS

The idea to write a book on the history of the city of Elkhart came to me during my research on the subject. I discovered that there were three comprehensive books on Elkhart County, but none on the city itself other than the booklet, *Taproots of Elkhart History,* (which is a valuable, accurate collection of newspaper articles written by Emil Anderson, and published in the *Elkhart Truth).* I have found that it is not possible to include everyone or every subject of interest concerning Elkhart. To do so would require several volumes. Even though every effort has been made by me and the advisory committee to insure historical accuracy and detail, in many cases information has been sketchy or contradictory. I apologize for any omissions or inaccuracies.

It is my desire to dedicate this book to my wife, Maija, for all her love, support, and editing, and to our two sons, Karl and Kevin, who have also supported my efforts in writing this book (including helping me learn how to operate a word processor).

Many individuals and organizations have helped make this book a reality. The countless hours of painstaking editing by my wife, Maija, have been crucial to the quality of the finished product. A great deal of help in providing pictures, ideas, and historical details came from my advisory committee members, Betty Flitcraft, Randy Adams, Terry Smeltzer, and especially Virginia Fluke, who spent many extra hours tracking down needed bits of information. I wish to thank Charles Brownewell and his commercial photography students at the Elkhart Area Career Center, and Rex Gleim, Director of Media Services for the Elkhart Community Schools, for their assistance. Thanks also go to Bettie East for her foreword, Scott Hendrie for his cover artistry, Brad Baraks for his helpful suggestions, patience, and guidance, and Ameritrust National Bank for their sponsorship.

Finally, I wish to express appreciation to the following people for contributing pictures and information:

Randall Adams
Mrs. Floyd Angelo
Robert H. Blessing
Mrs. Russell Boss
Mrs. Frank Bowen
Dr. James Broadbent
Mr. & Mrs. John Brumbaugh
Edward Chester
Mrs. Evelyn Clouse
Mrs. Owen Davis
Noble Detwiler
Elkhart Public Library
The *Elkhart Truth*
Carter Elliott
Betty Flitcraft
Virginia Fluke
Mrs. Mildred Fulwider
Rex Gleim
Mrs. William Heinhuis

Mrs. Lauraine Holycross
H. M. Jellison
John Jesse
Allen Kendall
Mrs. Forrest Kiebel
Sonya Long
William Lyzen
Rev. George Minnix
Mrs. M. C. Munford
Ralph Murphy
Mrs. John Nusbaum
Ruth Sager
Robert Schell
Jack & Beverly Shreiner
Terry Smeltzer
Dorothy Stocker
Paul Thomas
Jodie Trimmer
H. G. "Red" Truex
David Yoder

and many others.

The Advisory Committee for this book consisted of (from left to right): Betty Flitcraft, Terry Smeltzer, Randall Adams, and Virginia Fluke.

BIBLIOGRAPHY AND OTHER REFERENCES

A History of CTS Corporation 1896-1986, James H. Soltow, 1988.

A Standard History of Elkhart County Indiana, Abraham E. Weaver, 1916.

A Twentieth Century History and Biographical Record of Elkhart County, Indiana, Anthony Deahl, 1905.

Baptist Indian Missions, Rev. Isaac McCoy, 1842.

Centennial Edition, *Elkhart Truth,* September 13, 1958.

Centennial Section, *Elkhart Truth,* October 20, 1989.

City With A Heart, Marguerite Burkholder, 1958.

Elkhartans in 1880: Sketches for a Portrait, Martha M. Pickrell, 1979.

Elkhart Centennial Souvenir Program, May 1958.

Elkhart City Directories, 1860-present.

Elkhart Daily Review, Special Edition, May 27, 1910.

Elkhart on the Old St. Joe, Chamber of Commerce, 1923.

Elkhart Truth, Special Edition, September 26, 1900.

Elkhart Truth, Special Edition, 1910.

Elkhart Truth, Special Edition Progress Number, October, 1924.

Flitcraft Scrapbooks (14 volumes), Betty Flitcraft, 1983-89.

For Land Sakes, 73 Years in Real Estate, Charles H. Fieldhouse, 1957.

Historical articles in The *Elkhart Truth* by First National Bank, 1921-24.

History of Elkhart County Indiana, Charles C. Chapman, 1881.

Jottings About the Sedate Eighties and the Gay Nineties, Polly Bently, July, 1938.

Local history reference index file, Elkhart Public Library.

Local newspapers on microfilm, 1859-present.

Manual of Elkhart, George W. Butler, 1889.

Miles 1884-1984, A Centennial History, William C. Cray, 1984.

New Home Souvenir of the *Elkhart Truth,* 1918.

100 Years of Elkhart High School, 1872-1972, John A. Stinespring, 1972.

Pictorial and Biographical Memoirs of Elkhart and St. Joseph Counties, Goodspeed Brothers, 1893.

Pictorial Review of the Police Department, 1914.

Pioneer History of Elkhart County, Henry S. K. Bartholomew, 1930.

Planning Projects for Elkhart, Indiana, John Nolan and Philip W. Foster, 1923.

Police and Fire Guide, 1924.

Recollections of Early Elkhart, E. J. Davis, St. Jo River Pilot, 1841.

Second Street in Retrospect, Ethel Savage, 1958.

Souvenir Edition of the Metropolitan Police Department, 1925.

Stories and Sketches of Elkhart County, Henry S. K. Bartholomew, 1936.

Taproots of Elkhart History, Emil V. Anderson, 1949.

Winey Books (Numbers 1-10), Austin Winey, 1920's.

Women in Elkhart a Century Ago, Martha M. Pickrell, 1978.

All the above references may be found at the Elkhart Public Library, 300 South Second Street, Elkhart.

Other Sources:

Elkhart City Historical Researchers.

Elkhart County Historical Museum, 304 West Vistula, Bristol.

Miles Archives, Randolph and Michigan streets, Elkhart.

Ruthmere Museum, 302 East Beardsley Avenue, Elkhart.

"Time Was" Museum, Paul Thomas, 125 North Main Street, Elkhart.

Index

OUR HANDS
serve you gladly

OUR MINDS
plan that good food

OUR HEARTS
welcome you to Woody and Irma's